Imagining the End of Life in Post-Enlightenment Poetry

Florida A&M University, Tallahassee
Florida Atlantic University, Boca Raton
Florida Gulf Coast University, Ft. Myers
Florida International University, Miami
Florida State University, Tallahassee
University of Central Florida, Orlando
University of Florida, Gainesville
University of North Florida, Jacksonville
University of South Florida, Tampa
University of West Florida, Pensacola

Imagining the End of Life
in Post-Enlightenment Poetry

Voices against the Void

David J. Gordon

University Press of Florida
Gainesville/Tallahassee/Tampa/Boca Raton
Pensacola/Orlando/Miami/Jacksonville/Ft. Myers

Copyright 2005 by David J. Gordon
Printed in the United States of America on recycled, acid-free paper
All rights reserved
10 09 08 07 06 05   6 5 4 3 2 1

A record of cataloging-in-publication data is available from the
Library of Congress.
ISBN 0-8130-2865-5

The University Press of Florida is the scholarly publishing
agency for the State University System of Florida, comprising
Florida A&M University, Florida Atlantic University, Florida
Gulf Coast University, Florida International University, Florida
State University, University of Central Florida, University
of Florida, University of North Florida, University of South
Florida, and University of West Florida.

University Press of Florida
15 Northwest 15th Street
Gainesville, FL 32611-2079
http://www.upf.com

Contents

1

Imagining the End of Life

Until the emergence in early nineteenth-century Europe of what we would now call an existential view of death, the end of an individual life was an event whose significance was bound up inextricably with the interests and beliefs of a community. We now tend to think of a life as framed by birth and death, and to judge its success in terms of self-fulfillment. But during most of human history people understood their own lives as links in an ongoing chain, and thought of the work they did as tasks assigned rather than independently chosen. Individual death was thus part of a greater order of things, of some purpose that extended beyond the span of a single existence. Although sorrowful and solemn, it could not be reduced to an abrupt cessation of consciousness, a mere void. Rather, it was imagined as a change from a more definite to a less definite state of being, from "life" to some version of an "afterlife."

Afterlife mythologies are certainly part of the two major cultural traditions, the Greco-Roman and the Judeo-Christian, that have most strongly influenced Western poetry down to the present time. This study will take as its point of departure the fact that these mythologies have lost much of their authority since the Enlightenment, but their residual place in our imaginative consciousness should be acknowledged at the outset. The dramatic Christian version of the afterlife, featuring divine judgment, heaven, hell, and redemption from death, is still familiar, in large part because it has been so lavishly represented in visual and literary art. The Jewish version may be distinguished from the Christian by its less eschatological and otherworldly emphasis, but it has nourished similarly consoling beliefs. Psalm 49, for example, refers to God redeeming a soul from the power of the grave, and Psalm 16 touches on the idea of resurrection. Also, the Jewish prayer for the dead known as the Kaddish, medieval in origin though now a respected element of an ongoing tradition, speaks of a vaguely future time when the meaning of grief will be known, and observant Jews recite it to prepare the dead for reunion with God.[1]

The Greco-Roman religion lacked the notion of salvation and lacked as well any belief in a power beyond the grave that rewards and punishes the dead, but it too included a mythic state beyond life, an underworld. The Greeks took seriously the idea that the dead retained certain legal rights and could experience reunion with the living, even receive gifts and messages from them.[2] They pitied rather than feared their dead (picturing them typically as dim and strengthless bodies, never as corpses or skeletons), reluctant to believe that bodies were ever entirely cut off from the living spark, the psyche or soul. Achilles in the underworld rejects the consolation of visiting Odysseus, saying he would prefer to live servile on earth than rule over shades. The scene captures the Greek sense that death, while certainly inferior to life, is yet a kind of life. The same inference may be drawn from Plato's *Phaedo*, where Socrates reasons at some length that, since the soul seems to be immortal, a man should be cheerful as he enters Hades.

Throughout the Middle Ages, Greco-Roman and Judeo-Christian iconographies regarding the dead were similar enough that they could be joined without strain.[3] Moreover, and this is the point of present importance, both traditions have undergone similar challenge and suffered similar attrition from the influence of science and secularism advancing in the wake of Enlightenment.

In view of the fact that a certain amount of rationalistic skepticism about an afterlife, notably among the Epicureans and Stoics, is also part of classical tradition, we may wonder whether poets in particular believed in these mythologies or whether they merely made use of them. Did not some poets even in ancient times write about the afterlife in a skeptical spirit?[4] And isn't an imaginary existence beyond death even today a poetic option, as in Seamus Heaney's *Station Island*? Yes to both questions, and yet there is a difference. Even the most sophisticated representatives of the classical world, like Plato and Aristotle, did not sharply distinguish, as we do, between mythical beliefs and hypotheses requiring verification. As a result, even when death was understood as in some sense a final event, the nothingness that lay beyond it did not seem quite meaningless. Indeed, the idea of a truly meaningless void in connection with the cessation of consciousness seems to have developed only during the last two hundred years and to have done so only by degrees.

Further comment is in order about the particular case of Lucretius (whose *De Rerum Natura* derives from Epicurus), if only because his big poem makes much of "the void." It is worth remarking initially that the influence of Epicurus-Lucretius surged during the nineteenth century, notably marking the skeptical thinking of Shelley, Schopenhauer, Leopardi, Büchner, Emerson, Whitman, Nietzsche, Santayana, and Stevens. More directly pertinent is the fact that the void of Lucretius has little to do with death, serving rather to explain in materialist terms how the motion of physical bodies is possible. The void was for him a something enabling such motion. If we understand the word to mean nothing at all, what Lucretius meant is quite different. He does, to be sure, get around (in book 3) to enlarging on the idea that the fear of death should not touch us inasmuch as the mind is but a mortal possession and we shall have no mind to fear with after death. Accordingly, both the Epicureans and the Stoics of the classical world (and later humanists like Erasmus who were influenced by them) made a concerted effort to subdue the fear of death by way of reason. But this is not quite the modern view of the matter.

Although the argument is still made that our fear of death, being irrational, is unworthy of respect, the stronger argument today is that this fear looks different when we take our emotional life into account. The Nobelist J. M. Coetzee in his recent book *Elizabeth Costello* provides a particularly vivid instance of this modern point of view: "When I know . . . that I am going to die . . . what I know is what a corpse cannot know: that it is extinct, that it knows nothing and will never know anything any more. For an instant, before my whole structure of knowledge collapses in panic, I am alive inside that contradiction, dead and alive at the same time."[5] Coetzee is able to make us see for a moment—which is all we can bear—what we think feelingly about being dead.

Post-Enlightenment poetic consciousness is marked by the insight that this fear, although no longer complicated and magnified by a widespread belief in a punishing hell, cannot be reasoned into submission, because our own death, except as an abstract idea, is unimaginable.

Freud gives us a psychological version of this important insight, Wittgenstein a logical version, and Kenneth Burke a literary version, and each is crucial for the argument presented in the following pages.

"Our own death," Freud wrote, "is indeed unimaginable, and whenever we make the attempt to imagine it we can perceive that we really survive as spectators. Hence the psycho-analytic school could venture on the assertion that at bottom no one believes in his own death, or to put the same thing in another way, in the unconscious every one of us is convinced of his own immortality."[6]

Here are a few literary applications of this insight. Jules Laforgue began a poem called "The Impossible" with the line "Tonight I may die" and went on to imagine fellow-feeling proceeding from the stars whose future motions (he concludes) "I will not have been among." A similar example is "The Day of My Death" by Pier Paolo Pasolini, a poem that pictures a boulevard in the Friulian spring sunshine and "beautiful boys / [who] will run in that light / which I've just lost." Fine as these poems are, a reader cannot miss the spark of self-pity that sets them aglow. That is, the kind of pathos they generate derives from the continuing presence on the scene of the speaker-poet. One more example, slightly different, is the "Will" drafted by Michael Henchard in Thomas Hardy's *The Mayor of Casterbridge*. It concludes: "& that no murners [sic] walk behind me at my funeral. / & that no flours [sic] be planted on my grave. / & that no man remember me." Again we cannot miss the speaker's self-satisfying contemplation of his own obliteration, although in this case we infer that Hardy himself meant to convey this understanding while his fictional character is unaware of it.[7]

Ludwig Wittgenstein phrased his version of the insight in question with logical acuity:

> Death is not an event in life. Death is not lived through. If by eternity is understood not endless temporal duration but timelessness, then he lives eternally who lives in the present. Our life is endless in the way that our visual field is without limit. The temporal immortality of the human soul, that is to say, its eternal survival after death, is not only in no way guaranteed, but this assumption in the first place will not do for us what we always tried to make it do. Is a riddle solved by the fact that I survive forever? Is this eternal life not as enigmatic as our present one?[8]

This analysis calls attention to the intractable logical problem involved in trying to imagine what is "not an event of life," what is "not lived through." It does not fall into the rationalistic trap of inferring that, because death is unknowable, the mystery (and hence the fear) of it disappears. "Eternal life" can be called mysterious—Wittgenstein describes it as "enigmatic"—but it is mysterious or enigmatic only in the same sense that our present life is. One recalls the shrewd riposte to the familiar observation that life is strange: "as compared with what?"[9]

Kenneth Burke phrased the insight we are discussing in such a way as to call our attention to the indirection that poets must employ if they would write about the end of their own lives:

So far as the world of our positive experience is concerned, death can only be an idea, not something known by us as we know our bodily sensations. In fact, its ideality is probably one element that recommends it to the use of poets whose trade is to deal exclusively in symbols. . . . Moreover, since no poet can write of death from an immediate experience of it, the imagining of death necessarily involves images not directly belonging to it. It lies beyond the realm of images—or at least beyond the realm of such images as the living body knows.[10]

Burke's analysis goes a step beyond Freud and Wittgenstein in noting that "the imagining of death necessarily involves images not directly belonging to it." This brings us back to the problem of the poet, especially the poet living in an age that has absorbed this insight.

I think there are three ways in which poets may deal with (since they cannot dismiss) the problem posed by Burke, the last two of which are implied by his statement. The first is to acknowledge, through the use of ironical wit, that the intent to "imagine death" cannot be carried out literally. Here are several examples. William Empson concludes his witty poem "Ignorance of Death" with the lines: "I feel very blank upon this topic, / And think that though important, and proper for anyone to bring up, / It is one that most people should be prepared to be blank upon."[11] Then there is Samuel Beckett's Estragon looking around an empty stage, a stage that for Beckett represents either life or death, and punning balefully, "no lack of void." And, third, we may recall the drollery of Tom Stoppard's Rosencrantz and his baffled meditation on the afterlife: "Eternity is a terrible thought. I mean, where is it going to end?" (I will pursue this topic a little further in chapter 5 in connection with Philip Larkin's poem "Aubade.")

A second way around the problem of imagining death is suggested by Burke's phrase, "images not directly belonging to it." Poets have always evoked the world of death through images of silence, motionlessness, darkness, emptiness, or coldness, often in connection with earth, sea, and sky. Modern poetry does so as well, but what is distinctive about modern poetic consciousness is its more overt awareness of the metaphorical nature of such imagery, the tendency to place images within a naturalistic frame of reference and to divest them of otherworldly connotation.

My original title for this study was "Imagining Death in Post-Enlightenment Poetry," but when I realized that I would always think of the phrase "Imagining Death" in quotation marks because death cannot be experienced (although it can be abstractly or ideally acknowledged), I changed it to

"Imagining the End of Life." The ambiguity of the new phrase proved welcome. It continued to suggest death, but it also pointed to a position within life from which we view the prospect of death. This shift of emphasis away from knowledge that cannot be experienced is crucially important in modern poetry.[12]

A third way round the problem is implied by Burke's mention of the fact that poets are attracted to the subject of death because of its very ideality. Beyond the realm of images lies what we are obliged to call nothingness or void, words that introduce an existential view of death. But nineteenth- and twentieth-century poetry about the end of life, unlike earlier poetry, is ready to question the concept of void directly, in an attempt to generate some intellectual energy by doing so.

My book is organized so as to trace the literary development of the existential attitude toward death. After a chapter that surveys the seeding of the idea during the early modern centuries culminating in the Enlightenment, I devote the greater part of this study to what I take to be the three successive phases of its development during the last two centuries, three poetic approaches to the end of life, after death has begun to be understood as the end of individual consciousness, no longer as something lived through and therefore part of life.

Before describing these phases, however, I must take a moment to clarify the sense in which I am using the words "nothingness" and "void" because another usage that has currency may cause some confusion. The philosopher Martin Heidegger speaks for that other usage when he raises the old question "Why is there any being at all and not rather Nothing?"[13] In so doing he is ascribing to his *Nichts* a kind of mystic penumbra. One must encounter, he would say, the reality of Nothing in order to know Being in a more mysterious and profound sense than that of mere existence. Of course, poets and philosophers are entitled to invoke the word in some such sense. Rilke (of whom I will speak later in this chapter) does so, and Nietzsche's void is sometimes rather mysterious too, even though Nietzsche is fairly regarded as an early existentialist. I am not trying to argue against this usage, only to explain that I shall use the terms "nothingness" and "void" in a more concrete and limited sense: namely, the cessation of consciousness. This void may be called meaningless because it is unimaginable. From a Wittgensteinian point of view, it is beyond the reach of language that searches for truth on the basis of evidence, though it remains intelligible as the expression of religious belief, based on subjective faith rather than objective evidence.[14]

I can clarify a little further what I am getting at by widening the historical lens and contrasting the medieval Christian denial of the void with the contemporary poet's and thinker's denial of it on grounds so directly opposite that the two pictures resemble one another. C. S. Lewis wrote of a principle of plenitude that governed the medieval mind. No corner of the cosmos, or indeed of any map of the world, could truly be empty for medieval man because the divine spirit filled everything and dwelled everywhere. For a philosopher like Wittgenstein, on the other hand, or for a poet like John Ashbery, the void is again meaningless because we cannot think the cessation of thinking, and our effort to do so merely projects outward the stuff of our own consciousness. In John Ashbery's words, "It could be that time and space are filled with these [random perceptions and words], that there is no such thing as a void, only endless lists of things that one may or may not be aware of . . . pointless diversity."[15] We see, then, that a void completely filled with meaning and one completely emptied of meaning bear a curious resemblance to one another.

With the profound shift of sensibility introduced by the turn from Enlightenment to Romanticism, socially cohesive religious myths of the afterlife became insecure and were replaced, though not all at once or without resistance. Replaced by what? Some major poets of the Romantic period explored the new sense of closeness between the very words "life" and "death." At the same time, a Gothic tradition eroticized the void, and a more sophisticated Promethean tradition, which will be my principal concern in chapter 3, endeavored to confront an awesome blankness heroically. Byron's Death, Leopardi's *nulla*, and Jan Potocki's *Néant* are but three names for the Romantic void that inspired heroic confrontation. From Byron to Brontë, Death or Nothing was the kind of presence (capitalized as a rule) that stimulated challenge. Opposing the Void became a test of moral heroism, and I think it deserves to be understood as an incipient existentialism, anticipating the term that has become current since the 1940s.

In chapter 4, I mark out a long second phase of post-Enlightenment poetry that focuses on the end of life, extending from Tennyson and Dickinson down to Yeats and Lawrence. These poets were increasingly aware both of the declining influence of religion and of the consequential emptiness of death, which threatened their self-esteem, their confidence in human dignity. They were spurred accordingly to devise alternative—and necessarily idiosyncratic—conceptions of an afterlife, conceptions that indirectly acknowledged the agnostic spirit of the age without quite yielding to it. The philosophic thrust behind this phase, whether recognized or not, was that of

Nietzsche, who perceived that human beings were not well able to tolerate the removal of a higher purpose for life. But bold spirits, Nietzsche argued, could seize upon nihilism as a creative opportunity. Yeats's claim that we will see "the void grow fruitful" when we realize "we have nothing" is a characteristic instance of this sensibility, for which my heading is "Modifying the Void."

I will sometimes refer to aspects of this and the following phase of post-Enlightenment poetry as "post-Romantic." But I use this term only for the purpose of suggesting that these phases develop from the existential consciousness that broke into the open during the Romantic period. It need not compete with what we are accustomed to call by specific period names. The term is occasionally useful as a way of pointing simultaneously to the advance of religious agnosticism and to the heightened desire to create a substitute for it by way of individual myth.

The third and last phase of modern imagining of the end of life, studied in chapter 5, can be aligned with the philosophy of Wittgenstein, for whom the idea of immortality is indistinguishable from (though no less puzzling than) the mortal life we lead. This does not mean that contemporary poets have ceased to fear death or ceased to lift their voices "against" it. But the phrase "against the void" acquires a different meaning as the difficulty of imagining death comes to be more accepted. In my third and fourth chapters, "against" means opposed to or making use of, but in the fifth it means something like "leaning next to" and involves a shift of attention from death itself to the prospect of death. And this change of meaning entails a corresponding shift of the effect aimed at by modern poetry concerned with the end of life. It is poetry that, as Jahan Ramazani says about the modern elegist, "tends not to achieve but to resist consolation."[16] Opposition to and modification of the void, since they are courageous but not quite triumphant responses, involved a measure of heroic pathos, but poetry since the middle of the twentieth century has largely sacrificed the heroic stance, seeking a subtler mode of consolation.

I will have more to say about this subtler consolation at the end of the present chapter, but it is worth observing now that what I mean by the absence of traditional consolation in twentieth-century poetry is basically what David Bromwich means when he writes of the remarkable omission of "overt argument" in that poetry, its avoidance of "dramatic climax, or any moral to capitalize the significance of the incident [described]."[17]

My frame of reference throughout this study is literary-critical and is primarily concerned with the kind of poetry that speaks of private rather than public experience, with how poets, on our behalf, seem to talk to themselves. But since death is obviously a subject of broad cultural concern, I must in this opening chapter set my argument into a wider context. I am assuming that we have both a social and a private voice in the way we think and feel about death. The social voice within us is concerned with matters like legacy, inheritance, and reputation; it is responsive to our awareness that our lives will exert some influence on others even after our deaths. Similarly, the various customs people follow in regard to the deaths of others—involving funerary practice, mourning, and so forth—are aspects of their social consciousness. These arrangements and practices have changed considerably during the last century or two as a result of the same broad changes in the direction of privatization and secularization that have affected poetry. Therefore, taking notice of what cultural historians have to say about these changes will help us place more accurately the private voice that speaks within us as if unconscious of an audience, the voice we hear above all in lyric poetry. This is the voice that J. S. Mill (in his early essay "What is Poetry?") judged to be not so much heard as "overheard" and that John Keats admired because it could "strike the Reader as a wording of his own highest thoughts, and appear almost a Remembrance" (letter of 27 February 1818).

Following his work on the history of childhood, Philippe Ariès along with his colleagues undertook a comprehensive history of private life, and he then wrote several books on Western attitudes toward death since the Middle Ages. The nub of the later argument is that death, once regarded with awe and faced with dignity, has, in our day and in the industrial West especially, lost all moral significance. Before World War I, he asserted in *The Hour of Our Death* (*L'homme devant la mort* in the original French), "the death of a man still solemnly altered the space and time of a social group." Today, by contrast, influenced by medical technology and by our wish to render death invisible and no longer an evil, it has become "a biological transition without significance, without pain or suffering, and ultimately without fear."[18]

Sharp questioning of this argument has come from a French philosopher, Bernard Rousset, and an American historian, Paul Robinson. They do not dispute the general observation that social practices concerning death and dying have become secularized and privatized, hence that the religious and communal importance of death is now diminished. But they do query the tone of regret and dismay with which Ariès accompanies this observation. Rousset's contrary position is summarily stated in an essay pointedly titled

"La philosophie devant la mort": "a true philosophical lucidity should recognize that death and the dead are nothing and hold no significance at all."[19] Robinson raises a similar objection: "I disagree with Ariès's proposition that death is one of the great existential truths whose reality we must constantly reaffirm. The neglect of death, and its reduction to the insignificance of an ordinary event is, I would argue, a measure of our psychic maturity."[20]

Ariès laments our lost awe of death whereas his critics welcome it, but, as Robinson's comment makes clear, this is more than a debate about tone. My own position regarding the substance of the debate cannot be aligned with that of either party. Surely Rousset and Robinson go too far in suggesting that, influenced by secularization and modern medicine, the fear of death has mostly disappeared or, at least, should disappear. There remains for poets inclined to meditate on such matters something stubbornly incompatible with human desire about the inevitability of death. Indeed, some who recognize the new "insignificance" of death find a theme in the very discrepancy between our feeling about the subject and our rational understanding of it. Doubtless the fear of death has changed character with the virtual disappearance of heaven and hell.[21] But it is still quietly insistent. It goes without saying that an extreme fear of death is unhealthy and that different temperaments are differently susceptible to it, yet literary critics cannot ignore the fact that our poetry has been challenged by the conception of a meaningless void and has developed new styles of response to it.

Ariès himself did not quite ignore the evidence of the arts. In the last pages of his last book, *Images of Man and Death*, he made some effort to acknowledge the artistic response, but the effort was reluctant and incomplete. He began his conclusion with this assertion: "Relegated to the secret, private space of the home or the anonymity of the hospital, death no longer makes any *sign* [emphasis in the original]."[22] Then he turned to the cinema and, using two examples—Ingmar Bergman's *Cries and Whispers* and Claude Santel's *Les choses de la vie*—found symbolism lurking "beneath the silence of social practice." Without any appeal to divine or communal support, Bergman's servant offers the warmth of life to her dying mistress, and the waters in which Santel's drowning man "is about to disappear are irresistibly reminiscent of the primordial ocean . . . and the protective fluids of the womb." From these instances he inferred that "a new symbolism . . . appears to be forming tentatively around the modern idea of nothingness. However, this nothingness is not the pure abstraction of Robinson and Rousset. This nothingness has both time and space [and so proves] the power of the sign."[23] This surely is too timid. In his eagerness to rebut

Robinson and Rousset, Ariès turns only to a couple of cinematic narratives, a form designed for a wide audience in which the social voice presses forward. And what he finds, not surprisingly, is rather traditional symbolism of comfort beyond the grave. He is right that "the power of the sign" lives on, but he misses the point that the modern nothingness, for the advanced poet at any rate, cannot wear the old garb. The sign has moved on, sometimes using the old imagery but in a new way.

If contemporary poetry seems to find the subject of one's own death newly insignificant, I think this is because the significance we are accustomed to attach to this subject is expressed by way of overt statement and explicit consolation. Hugo von Hofmannstahl's early play "Death and the Fool" featured a character called Death who at the play's end leaves the stage shaking his head, bewildered by these strange (*wundervoll*) human creatures who "still find meaning in what is meaningless."[24] What Hofmannstahl's "Death" did not foresee is that poets would learn to make meaningful use of the idea of meaninglessness. To sharpen the paradox, our poets (beginning with the Romantics and in the twentieth century more directly) have learned to think and write about death not as a state of being but as a problem of consciousness involving the prospect of no longer being able to think and write. This is not what Hofmannstahl meant, but perhaps his words can be turned in that direction if, with a bit of license, we translate *wundervoll* as "wonderful" instead of "strange."

The last poem I will analyze in the chapters ahead, Jorie Graham's "Against Eloquence," serves as a paradigmatic example of this contemporary enterprise. Eloquence may be understood as precisely what a poet might bring to the subject of death and dying. But in Graham's poem it is a word for our hectic and desperate activity to blot out the void even though (or because) we recognize that the void of death can yield no meaning. No private meaning at any rate. When the poet Czeslaw Milosz writes that "to be meaningful, a death must be part of someone's life,"[25] I do not really disagree with him because he is referring to the social rather than the private voice we bring to the subject. Milosz's statement makes sense in relation to elegy, a social form of lyric.

Only chapter 5 concerns this latest stage of poetic consciousness. But the preceding chapters are also important. They show how this awareness has *developed,* how it is part of a longer story. Chapter 2 sets the stage for post-Enlightenment thought by tracing the origin of the modern idea from the early Renaissance through the Enlightenment. François Villon is seen to be the first important Western poet to express the sense of what Ariès calls "mort de soi" (one's own death) as something distinct from general human mortality. After Villon, I proceed to the pioneering writers of the later Renaissance, a time when the notion of a subjective self emerges distinctly. Seventeenth-century writers in particular began to see individual life as belonging to a private as well as public sphere, and to perceive (not without anxiety) a separation between individual and traditional religious thought. I touch in these pages on Ronsard, Montaigne, Shakespeare, Donne, Pascal, and Milton to illustrate the emergence, though not yet the centrality, of subjectivity. Rousseau's contribution is a fitting climax to this chapter because his thinking, in its depth and influence, establishes much of the groundwork for an existential view of the end of life. Rousseau did not preach against particular religious and social forms that supported people in the face of death, but his passionate advocacy of individual feeling as the source of true moral authority went far toward undermining their authority.

In chapter 3, "Opposing the Void: The Romantic Period," I touch on the work of various poets, novelists, and essayists but focus on Byron's *Manfred* and *Cain,* Shelley's *Frankenstein,* and Brontë's *Wuthering Heights* because these larger imaginative works make more explicit the new view of death implied in lyric. They help us map out and dramatize the conceptual innovation that is at work not only in this but also in the following chapters.

The self-conscious pioneers of the Romantic period were the first to be faced squarely with the idea of human existence as unsupported by anything beyond itself. But, as if taken by surprise, they included in this difficult and courageous confrontation certain defensive strategies. Wordsworth hints at a something beyond "human fears." Percy Shelley in a few poems infuses the idea of annihilation with a metaphysical aura. More typically, the Romantics dramatized an incipient existentialist position both by capitalizing the words "Death," "Nothingness," and "Void" and by heroicizing the consciousness that confronts them as presences. The tendency to endow the void they opposed with presence suggests that these early existentialists were not quite ready to replace the traditional afterlife with an unresponsive blank. But their confronting the void as they did certainly led subsequent poetry away from the traditional religious understanding of the end of life.

Chapter 4, "Modifying the Void: Mid-Nineteenth to Mid-Twentieth Century," examines in some detail the work of five poets—Tennyson, Dickinson, Housman, Yeats, and Lawrence—who found it harder than the Romantics did to get away from a developing spirit of science-inspired agnosticism, but who, rather than opposing the void directly, turned it to account, making it respond in one way or another to their creative need. All of these poets retained some attraction to a Christian understanding of an afterlife yet resisted Christian doctrine and worked out alternative myths in highly independent fashion. Aware of a progressive spirit in the air, they knew there was no turning back to a pre-existential view of death, yet all resourcefully sought to salvage some portion of the Christian tradition in forming their original poetic myths.

The progressive spirit in the nineteenth-century air was political and social as well as scientific. The specific belief in social and political progress that arose in the eighteenth century and flourished during the nineteenth and early twentieth centuries has, in fact, often been traced to the eschatology of Christian faith. Through the work of such writers as Hegel and Marx, Christian faith, it has been plausibly argued, was displaced onto history, whose inevitable progress would "redeem" society by revolution, establishing a heaven on earth. Even when not quite so visionary, Victorian poetry was fascinated by what has been called "the trope of onwardness,"[26] whether this assumed a biological, sociopolitical, or spiritual form.

The dissolution of the myth of progress during the twentieth century—the difficulty in our time of imagining any kind of future at all—is perhaps the principal fact behind the difference between the post-Romantic imagining of the end of life studied in chapter 4 and the contemporary imagining analyzed in chapter 5. Probably what killed this myth, even more than the political failure of socialism, was the exponential advance of technology, bringing to the forefront of our minds what we now routinely call weapons of mass destruction. The Mexican poet and essayist Octavio Paz wrote that the new "technology constitutes a radical critique of the idea of progress," causing us to doubt the very meaning of the word inasmuch as it makes more likely not only advances in human welfare but also the possibility of human extinction.[27] Without confidence in a collective future, we see the inevitability of our death in a new light. Darwin had demonstrated nature's indifference to man, but it took a nuclear age to bring home to us the notion that our collective fate is imperiled by forces of our own making, although forces beyond individual control. Of course poets, like the rest of us, do not go about in a state of constant anxiety. They try to get what pleasure they can out of life, which includes making something that may have value for others, such as poems that assimilate a newly shaded awareness of the end of life.

The poets who will receive close attention in my final chapter are Wallace Stevens, Elizabeth Bishop, Philip Larkin, Denise Levertov, Czeslaw Milosz,

Anthony Hecht, and Jorie Graham. It is a list not meant to evince any inner coherence beyond providing the opportunity to demonstrate that a handful of mid- and later twentieth-century poets with different biases and styles can be grouped so as to illustrate the distinctive new contours of a particular subject matter. As these poets, like their Victorian predecessors, have spun off the legacy they have inherited, they have retreated from the post-Romantic commitment to onwardness and seek to accommodate instead the idea of a canceled future. All of them retain in different degrees some positive response to a religious view of life if not to formal belief, but the tone of their poems is perceptibly different from that of their predecessors—quieter, less theatrical, perhaps less ambitious.

I thought of naming this latter poetic phase "post-existential," but that phrase would be misleading. The difference is less a matter of substance than of tone. These poets may be said to find consolation not in explicit meaning but in the poise and style they are able to maintain in the absence of such meaning. But to say that their imagining of the end of life has more to do with style than idea is not the same as saying that it lacks moral implication. The phrase "the redress of poetry" as deployed by Seamus Heaney nicely captures the elusive relation between the aesthetic and the moral dimension of modern verse. Heaney defines "redress" as "the way [poetry] justifies its readers' trust and vindicates itself by setting its fine excess in the balance against all of life's inadequacies, desolations, and atrocities."[28]

A word more about the apparent absence of consolation in the "mort de soi" poetry of our age. As Heaney suggests, aesthetic qualities in themselves—style and tone, metaphorical finesse, the sound of sense—may provide a kind of consolation because they imply a measure of moral confidence. But I think there is something more to this matter that comes into view if we enlist the seemingly vague word "beauty." What we call beauty in poetry (I think the word in relation to the visual arts, if not to music, must be discussed differently) is not merely a subjective impression but also has a cognitive aspect. It is a word we may well use when a line or a passage suggests a seductive state of *desirelessness*, as expressed, for example, in Shakespeare's "We are such stuff/ As dreams are made on, and our little life/ Is rounded with a sleep." Freud's disciple Hanns Sachs, in his 1942 classic *The Creative Unconscious*, linked "beauty" with this paradoxical mental state and did not hesitate to say that it implied acceptance of our necessary death. However odd it sounds at first to connect beauty to the thought of death—a thought we normally find repellent and fearful—we are likely to forget how much strain and energy we spend in desiring and enduring life;

hence, it should not surprise us altogether that we may experience as "beautiful" the thought, if well expressed, of relaxing this strain—as long, of course, as the danger of actual death does not interfere with our response. This kind of consolation, at any rate, continues to be available in a secular age, for it does not involve our engagement with an afterlife mythology.

A study titled *Imagining the End of Life in Post-Enlightenment Poetry* will arouse certain expectations that I will not or cannot meet, so I must set them down here.

I will not be dealing with poems about death in its most violent and dramatic form, as in war, suicide, or genocide. To do so would raise all sorts of political, social, and psychological issues that could not possibly be accommodated in an already complex plan. So I must exclude war poets as distinguished as Wilfred Owen, poets of personal desperation as gifted as Sylvia Plath, and a holocaust poet like Paul Celan, obsessed by "the scream that never falls silent."

A second exclusion will be made of poems that speak of death primarily in a mystical sense. Rilke is a distinguished practitioner of such poems. Although he frequently used the word "*Tod*" along with its variants, he usually meant not the extinction of the physical body and of consciousness but, as he wrote in a letter about the *Duino Elegies,* "the side of life averted from us." "The true figure of life," he went on, "extends through both spheres . . . there is neither a here nor a beyond, but only a great unity, in which those creatures that surpass us, the 'angels,' are at home."[29] At the end of the first elegy, he even uses the word "*Leere*," but this emptiness, which the dead are said to inhabit, "enraptures, consoles, and helps us." It is a poem neither about mourning nor about immortality but about a mystical unity of here and beyond.

Perhaps the poem by Rilke that comes closest to dealing with the end of life in the sense of the phrase this study will pursue is "The Swan," but it is a revealing near-exception. The poem opens with a fine simile comparing "dying, this no longer being able / to hold to the ground we stand on every day" to "the swan's anxious letting himself down—: // into the waters. . . ." But it goes on to focus on the swan's recovery from those waters, "which gently accept him / and, as if happy and already in the past, / draw away under him, ripple upon ripple, / while he, now utterly quiet and sure / and ever more mature and regal / and composed, is pleased to glide." In other words, the poem is concerned not with death but with an aesthetic recovery from physical clumsiness, a recovery made dramatic by ingenious spacing and punctuation.[30]

A similar exclusion must be made of other kinds of poems that also use the word "death" metaphorically, as in many French poems that have influenced and been influenced by literary theory. Literary academics are by now accustomed to such statements as "There is no denying that writing is a form of death, originating in loss and reenacting death's ultimate unrepresentability." This sentence, as it happens, was written by Richard Stamelman, who was thinking of Maurice Blanchot and Roland Barthes. His book *Lost Beyond Telling: Representations of Absence in Modern French Poetry* is a virtual anthology of such formulations stretching from Baudelaire to Derrida.[31] The critic Garrett Stewart has concisely described their philosophic underpinning: "In postmodernism, death shifts from sheer terminus to its role as the disclosed ground of all figuration."[32] Although I cannot make use of such statements in the body of my book, I will find a place for them in my Concluding Remarks, where I stand back from the particular poems submitted to analysis and ask what the very activities of writing and reading mean in the economy of life.

Another exclusion involves the vast body of poems throughout history evoking and lamenting the mortal human condition, the passing of things, irrevocable loss. Because such poems are related to the death-of-self poems at the center of my concern, some will receive mention along the way. But I think that most poems about mortality in general can be distinguished fairly well from death-of-self poems in that they express the sentiments of the human race rather than those of an individual person thinking intimately about his or her death. The one kind is likely to be general in scope and poignant in tone; the other is usually personal and meditative. In my effort to focus on the latter kind of poem, I am guided by the words of one of André Malraux's characters in *The Royal Way*: "There is . . . no death. . . . There is only . . . me . . . me . . . who is going to die."[33]

Finally, I have made some effort to exclude the ample tradition of elegy, poems that mourn the death of others, although, again, poems of this description are near relations of and even overlap death-of-self poems to some degree and so will also receive ad hoc attention throughout this study. Modern elegiac poets also tend to write unsentimentally about consolation, but writing about the death of another is a somewhat different matter from writing about one's own death. For one thing, the death of another surely *is* "an event of life." Mourning *is* "lived through." Ramazani's book about the modern elegy is properly entitled *The Poetry of Mourning*. Mourning is an important subject and one that has received much attention in recent years from literary critics, but it stands to the side of the subject matter I have delimited. An earlier Ramazani book about Yeats, subtitled *Elegy, Self-Elegy, and the Sublime*, somewhat blurs this distinction by grouping elegy with "self-elegy."[34] Harold Bloom, in his recent book titled *Genius*, also makes use of the phrase "self-elegy." But the term seems to me awkward and even misleading. Can we without sentimentality evoke on our own behalf the kind of pathos we evoke on behalf of another? Can one mourn oneself? One laments one's losses, but can one *mourn* them?

One might suppose that Gerard Manley Hopkins thought and said so in the famous final lines of "Spring and Fall: To a Young Child": "It is the blight man was born for, / It is Margaret you mourn for." But this is to use the word "mourn" to mean a broad lamentation over mortality, a grieving over the recurrent phenomenon of evanescence symbolized by the falling leaves. It is unlike what we normally mean by mourning, which is specific grief over someone's death that runs a nonrecurrent course over time. I think Hopkins's bold use of the word in this poem succeeds because it is presented to us as the unprecedented and naively felt experience of a child.

A better test of my question "can one mourn oneself?" would be Shakespeare in the sonnets lamenting loss again and again in the personal voice of the lyric poet. Combing through these poems, we do not find the word "mourn" used in connection with the idea of personal loss. Rather, the poet laments or "moans" a loss, as in sonnet #30: "I moan the expense of many a vanished sight." Would one want to call these poems self-elegies? Yeats wrote superb poems moaning the expense of many a vanished sight, but I would prefer not to call them self-elegies. Elegy, in my view, describes an allied topic rather than one directly in my path.[35]

But again, from the broad perspective of my Concluding Remarks, where I stand back and think of death in relation to the very activities of writing and reading, the distinction between elegy and self-elegy loses its importance.

Seeding the Idea of Existential Death

Philippe Ariès makes a distinction between a premodern attitude toward death—resignation to the mortal condition of humanity, expressed in the phrase "Et moriemur" (we shall all die)—and an attitude developing after the twelfth century that anticipates "the importance given throughout the entire modern period to the self" and is expressed by another phrase, "la mort de soi" (one's own death).[1] Among the first poets to voice this new attitude were François Villon in the fifteenth century and Pierre de Ronsard in the sixteenth. Each is worth some comment at the outset of this chapter.

The 2,024 lines of Villon's *Testament* refer rather frequently to God, Jesus, and the Church—along with persons to whom the Villon of the poem proffers a half-mocking, half-earnest farewell. He is usually irreverent in regard to the Church and churchmen, although he does not see himself as opposed to or separated from the Christian scheme of things. Probably such a stance was not possible for him and, it has been argued, was not possible even for a sixteenth-century successor like Rabelais, whose satirical view of political and religious authority was still more robust.[2] Nonetheless, the authorial stance throughout the *Testament* is frank and fearless, free of both formalities and pieties, and boldly vernacular in style. Like Rabelais after him, Villon mixes scatology and religion without a trace of embarrassment.

The numerous references in the *Testament* to the prospect of death (Villon did in fact die—or disappear at least—two years after writing the poem, although he was only about thirty at the time) are influenced by both Greco-Roman and Christian traditions. The poet gives thanks for the pleasure he has enjoyed in life, deploys the *carpe diem* motif in lyrical *ballades*, and parades the spectacle of the body's decay. These themes were conventional enough in his day, but the poem's rhetoric at every point is energized by an individual voice. Its varying moods make up a whole that might be paraphrased as follows: By God, I enjoyed myself, but what a hard time I had, and now I am old at a young age, damn it all.

Villon was writing during a period described by Johan Huizinga, in his classic study *The Autumn of the Middle Ages,* as unique in the stress it laid on the thought of death. According to Huizinga, there were in the French and Netherlandish art of the fifteenth century "three themes that furnished the melody for the never ending lament about the end of earthly glory. First there was the motif that asked, where have all those gone who once filled the earth with glory? Then there was the motif of the horrifying sight of the decomposition of all that had once constituted earthly beauty. The last was the motif of the *danse macabre* or *Totentanz,* the dance of death which whirls away people of any age or profession."[3] Villon's poem certainly illustrates the first and second if not the third of these motifs, but it is scarcely morbid. (Its "new touch," according to Huizinga, was that of "gentle sorrow.")[4] It is much more about fate and fortune than about judgment, easily mixing classical figures like Diomede and Alexander with biblical and ecclesiastical ones to show the range of ill-fortune in human affairs. Moreover, the poet's remarkable mobility of mind sustains the liveliness of his individual voice. The "I" offers his soul to the glorious Trinity, his body to the earth, his library to his father, and to his mother these very words that may outlive his body. No money—the usual substance of a legacy—is bestowed because, we are told, it all went "to the taverns and the girls," for "there's no pleasure like living high." Villon ends with characteristic panache, calling his third-person protagonist a martyr—of an unusual kind: "For he died a martyr to love / This he swore on his testicle / As he made his way out of this world."[5]

The voice of Ronsard in the following century is less ribald and spiky, more conscious of the influences it makes use of and in its turn more influential, but insofar as Ronsard deals with personal material (which he does most notably in *Pièces posthumes* published a year after his death), the individuality of this voice is more intimate than Villon's. The readiest example of this remarkable intimacy in a poem about dying is "A son âme" ("To His Soul"), Ronsard's version of Emperor Hadrian's address to *his* dying soul. We can better appreciate its quality if we first set down, beside a translation, Hadrian's five lines:

Animula vagula blandula
Hospes comesque corporis

Quae nunc abibis in loca
Pallidula, rigida, nudula,
Nec, et ut soles, dabis iocos.

[Little wandering soul,
Guest and companion of my body,
Where are you going to now?
Away into bare, bleak places,
Never again to share a joke.][6]

This English translation does not quite capture the effect of those diminutives in the first and fourth lines of the original, but even the Latin lacks the tenderness that Ronsard brings to his subject:

Little soul, little Ronsard's,
Darling and delicate;
Precious hostess of my body,
You are going down there,
Weak, pale, thin, and lonely
Into the cold Kingdom of the dead.
Altogether simple, without remorse,
Hate, poison or rancor—
Mistrusting favor, wealth,
So longed for by others,
Pass on, I've spoken, follow your fortune,
Don't trouble my rest, now I sleep.[7]

The principal themes of the nine *Pièces posthumes* are the physical decay of the poet's own body, the psychological as well as physical pain of dying, the appeal to God for pity and to Death for sleep, a stoical resolve to face death according to the example of Christ, and a dignified regret for and pride in what must be left behind. Ronsard's handling of the first of these themes is especially original in view of the later emergence of existential death, and one of these poems should be quoted in full to illustrate his achievement:

I have nothing left but my bones, I am like a
    skeleton,
Without flesh, nerves, muscles, or pulp,
Struck by Death's unforgiving arrow,
I dare not look at my arms lest I tremble.
Apollo and his sons, both great masters,

Would not be able to heal me. Their profession has
    betrayed me.
Farewell pleasant sunshine! My eye is stopped up,
    My body is falling apart.
What friend, seeing me ravaged to this point,
Does not come with eyes sad and moist,
Consoling me in bed and kissing my face,
While wiping my eyes, which Death has put to sleep?
Farewell dear companions, farewell dear friends!
I shall go ahead and make a place for you.[8]

Not the poem of a man on the outs like Villon's *Testament*, it nonetheless turns the spectacle of decay into an exploration of subjectivity. Despite its conventional touches (Death's arrow, Apollo's betrayal, the farewell to friends), we do not doubt that what is described is a particular man's sense of his own physical decline. This impression comes partly from the way the frequent first-person pronouns are applied to a particular body and predicament, partly from the way repetition of sound and sense accumulates intensity, as in the second line of the original French ("decharné, denervé, demusclé, depoulpé"), well beyond what would be required merely to indicate the decay of flesh. It comes above all from the peculiar tenderness that the poet is able to convey toward his own body and situation, despite his dismay. He imagines friends who are not disgusted or aloof but who, with moist eyes, are "consoling me in bed and kissing my face." Giving intimacy to his conventional farewell gesture, he imagines himself in turn preparing for them a place in another world.

Ariès observed that "in the late middle ages the only inhabited space, the only space subject to the rule of law, was communal space."[9] But Ronsard's poem of the high Renaissance begins to carve out a private space from that of the community. Although neither Ronsard nor Villon opposed communal custom and belief in regard to death and dying, as pioneering writers of the Romantic period would do, each gave new importance to individual feelings and circumstances.

This new attitude gains depth and complexity in the work of such major writers of the sixteenth and seventeenth centuries as Montaigne, Shakespeare, Donne, Milton, and Pascal.

Montaigne is almost always ready with a classical reference but wants to think everything out afresh, taking himself as the primary source of wisdom. His meditations on death reflect the traditional concern with the mortal condition of man and man's moral preparation for death, but it is always the writer as a man individually circumstanced, a man concerned with his own aging, who is meditating. Simone de Beauvoir wrote of Montaigne: "using his own experience, he examined old age as if no one before him had ever spoken of it."[10] In so doing, he made a new subject of the writing self, inventing a genre that we still call by the name he created for it, the essay.

Shakespeare's impersonality is almost legendary, yet critics credit him with originating "the subjectivity effect," "the invention of the human," and "the means to represent inwardness."[11] I want to focus for a moment on what Hamlet in his third soliloquy and Claudio pleading with his sister in *Measure for Measure* have to say about the fear of death because these speeches offer a sharp pre-existentialist glance at the nothingness that nineteenth-century poets acknowledged as a new problem to be faced in an age after the philosophic underpinning of religion had weakened. Hamlet meditates on "the dread of something after death" that makes us "rather bear those ills we have / Than fly to others that we know not of." Claudio, with less dignity and more terror, successively imagines his unknowable death in terms of cold rot, fiery floods, terrible ice, violent winds, and the howling damned. One of the reasons why these speeches are so impressive is that Shakespeare has made Hamlet's dread and Claudio's fear palpable, and I call them pre-*existentialist* because Hamlet's "know not of" and Claudio's "know not where" anticipate what later writers mean by nothingness.

One would not call John Donne's evocation of death's fearful blankness in "A Hymn to God the Father" similarly pre-existentialist, even though it resembles Hamlet's and Claudio's in its intensity:

> I have a sin of fear, that when I have spun
> My last thread, I shall perish on the shore;
> But swear by thy self, that at my death thy son
> Shall shine as he shines now, and heretofore;
> And, having done that, Thou hast done,
> I fear no more.[12]

The foreboding expressed in the first two lines of this splendid stanza is resonant, but the speaker's fear of death is really fear of God's judgment and is, moreover, relieved by a punning confidence in the Son's redemptive power and the Father's acceptance of the sinner. This is not to suggest that explicit religious faith weakens a poem aesthetically, only that it prevents its possessing a pre-existentialist aura.

Indeed, the Shakespearean passages are no more than *pre*-existentialist because the fear expressed in them is not separate from the assumption that there *is something* after death and that this something is part of a vast though unknowable order of things. For Hamlet and Claudio, what follows death is unknowable but not unthinkable. It remains somewhat closer to the medieval idea of a God-filled void than to a modern idea of an afterlife that baffles thought and language.

One can perhaps better appreciate this aspect of Shakespeare's picture of nothingness by comparing it with the more obviously ironical picture provided by Milton's Belial in *Paradise Lost*. Belial, it will be remembered, argues against renewed war with God because, bad as things are, they could get worse. They could result in the cessation of consciousness: "To be no more, sad cure; for who would lose, / Though full of pain, this intellectual being, / Those thoughts that wander through eternity" (book 2: 145–48). Assigning Hamlet's and Claudio's fear to a cowardly devil, Milton makes it clear that the great order of things as understood by Shakespeare is undeniably there, and that it is ordained by God, not a human invention.

As the idea of individual death gains strength in the course of the seventeenth century, it is more difficult to isolate the contributions of particular writers and correspondingly more useful to describe broad tendencies. One way of formulating such tendencies is in terms of cultural history. Studying the cultural history of the period, Philippe Ariès selects three that seem salient. First, the increased intervention of the state in communal life made individuals more conscious of the family and the value of privacy. Second, the increase in literacy and the availability of books encouraged "silent reading" and reflection. And third, the dramatic emergence of Protestantism fostered "inward piety" and self-examination.[13] Each of these is immediately suggestive. The century's new interest in family life is reflected in its visual art; its new interest in reading is evidenced by a turn to diaries and letter writing; and a new regard for the privacy of religious experience is expressed through spiritual autobiographies and the growth of pietistic sects.

The third of the tendencies specified by Ariès—involving the Protestant Reformation and the Catholic reaction—has the most direct bearing on the emergent concern with individual death, if only because it indicates a potential resistance to the authority of church and state. So I want to develop it a little by way of the contrasting examples of Milton and Pascal.

Each of these great writers—the passionate Protestant and the passionate Jansenist—derived obvious and strong support from his version of the Christian religion, yet each was influenced by the spirit of the age to describe, for the believing Christian, a new sense of danger and isolation. Each implied that a new degree of effort was required to maintain faith. Like his Abdiel in *Paradise Lost,* Milton saw himself as a "Servant of God" who well hast . . . fought / The better fight, who single hast maintained / Against revolted multitudes the cause / Of truth" (book 6: 29–32). His strong faith in the "inner light" was matched by his readiness to subject religious and political institutions to vigorous questioning. The work of the Counter-Reformation thinker Pascal was directed toward a similar end. Although he did not seek to undermine the authority of priest and king, he was more daring than the Protestant writers in exploring man's *distance* from God, in exploring human isolation and despair. One remembers in the *Pensées* Pascal's fear of eternal silence in the universe and his linking of unhappiness with isolated privacy. Milton's strong faith in the inner light *seems* quite different from Pascal's deep suspicion of selfhood. But each writer was endeavoring, as a believing Christian, to conquer pride—Milton by disciplining it through allegiance to God, Pascal by dissolving it in the realization of God's inconceivable distance from man. Milton the Englishman dramatizes a moral victory emerging from psychological conflict. Pascal the Frenchman registers the shock of a logical contradiction that, by obliterating a middle ground, opens not only human despair but also the possibility, beyond our will, of divine grace.

The particular way that each brings passionate individual feeling into congruence with the will of God exhibits the strenuous work of a strong mind. But the general goal both were aiming at belongs broadly to their age. And this fact makes less surprising the emergence of a thinker like Rousseau who finds an original way (that requires not striving exactly but seeing differently) of bridging the separation between natural feeling and moral idealism, between "is" and "ought."

Probably the change of orientation at the end of the seventeenth and beginning of the eighteenth century that most clearly paves the way for Rousseau is the rise of historical consciousness. Before the Enlightenment, man's moral nature was assumed to be given and unchangeable, in effect ahistorical. Of course there had always been disagreement about the proportion of good and evil in the human soul and hence about the appropriate degree of discipline to be exerted by whatever political or religious authority happened to be in power. But although the wisdom or legitimacy of a particular political or religious authority was always subject to question, the legitimacy of such authority itself never was. Authority simply derived from God or, as in Plato, from some comparably absolute metaphysical ground. The idea that such authority was not absolute but historically contingent had not yet gained traction. The Chain of Being paradigm that prevailed through the Middle Ages and into the Renaissance assumed a fixed order of authority in human realms and in the cosmos at large. It was an order not subject to historical evolution or revolution.

The various causes that led to the rise of historical consciousness cannot be considered here, but certainly such a profound change of outlook as the one that climaxed so dramatically in the French Revolution was not the work of one man, although it will be useful in this survey to focus on the particular achievement of Jean-Jacques Rousseau. Let us approach it by observing that the question proposed by the Academy of Dijon in 1749, launching Rousseau's career—"Has the restoration of the sciences & arts tended to purify morals?"—already implies an assumption that we do not find in Shakespeare or Montaigne, Milton or Pascal: namely, that civilization itself is subject to question. We can detect some anxiety about civilization as early as the mid-seventeenth century in the *Leviathan* (1651) of Thomas Hobbes. Although Hobbes pays lip service to the deity, in effect he subordinates divine to civil authority, and it is on behalf of the latter that he is anxious. His treatise postulates that, without a firm and secure civil authority to regulate them, human beings would revert to a "state of nature" in which their unregulated competitiveness and greed would result in anarchy and mutual destruction.

Bernard Mandeville, in his early eighteenth-century *Fable of the Bees*, did not estimate human nature more flatteringly than did Hobbes, but he defended civilization by arguing that the irreducible clash of individual desires resulted, as in a beehive, in a socially functioning system. His thesis is summed up in his subtitle, "Private Vices, Publick Benefits," and again in the couplet "The worst of all the Multitude / Did something for the Common Good."[14] Rousseau read Mandeville and was greatly influenced by Hobbes, but these were pragmatic (if nervous) defenses of prevailing systems, whereas he was ready to question civilization itself, making way for a new, historical conception of human nature.

The two most important starting points for Rousseau were, first, Augustine's explanation of human nature and destiny in terms of Adam's fall, an event antedating and determining human history that was redeemed only by the advent of Christ, and, second, Hobbes's hypothesis of a lawlessly aggressive state of nature justifying the control and restraint of strong civil government. Rousseau zeroed in on each of these very influential ideas and turned each in a new direction.

I take up the second of them first. Yes, Rousseau agreed, let us postulate an original state of nature, but human beings were not fearful and vicious in it. Rather, this was a state of primitive simplicity in which we were free from conflict. Because our needs and powers were in balance, there was order and proportion and we were content. Being naturally good, we were ignorant of vice and had no need to strive for virtue. And yes, we may postulate a fall of man, but it occurred within history, as people forsook the state of nature for civilization and became corrupted by passions aroused from the outside, from a social source, from external stimuli that disquieted their imaginations. Civilization created a kind of false or unnatural self marked by "amour propre" (vanity), displacing a true or natural self marked by "amour de soi" (self-esteem). In decided contrast to Hobbes, Rousseau imagined the self in a state of nature to be concerned only with self-preservation, whereas the unhappy self in civil society was stirred up by envy, hostility, and fear of death. Evil, then, came into the world not with the first man but with civilization. "God makes all things good; man meddles with them and they become evil." Again, "[God made us] free and good. . . . It is the abuse of our powers that makes us wicked and unhappy."[15]

If evil arose from a change of circumstance rather than from human nature itself and if by a better understanding of our true needs we can correct the situation, then human beings are entirely responsible for moral change. This puts both human nature and human institutions in a new light. They are no longer given but have evolved; they are not fixed but alterable. Kant hailed Rousseau as a Newton of the mind because he removed God from moral arrangements as Newton removed God from physical arrangements yet kept him as a Creator concerned in a remote way with the order of the universe. The horrendous Lisbon earthquake of 1755 was a phenomenon seized on by Voltaire as evidence that there *were* natural evils, a very troubling thought for religious believers. But Rousseau roundly disputed this view of the matter, convinced that we accept natural evils and do not blame them on the deity.[16] By removing God from human arrangements, he is saying that justice is an altogether *human affair.* That is, religious and social institutions can make no appeal to a higher law. The revolutionary potential of such a position is obvious, and it was realized before the century's end.

What Rousseau required to energize his vision was a new moral center or guide, replacing the grounding afforded by religious and social beliefs and institutions. His favorite name for it is "nature," whose first impulses, according to the Savoyard Priest who speaks for Rousseau in *Emile,* "are always right." It is associated with "conscience," whose decrees "are not judgments but feelings." In turn, "conscience never deceives us . . . he who obeys his conscience is following nature." The authoritative Priest continues, "I know from experience that conscience persists in following the order of nature in spite of all the laws of man."[17]

We must not miss, however, the polarized character of Rousseau's moral vision. It tells us that an original rightness subsists in the human heart as a core of natural feeling but also that we abuse our powers and thus are afflicted with a fatal wrongness. We can therefore describe it as either optimistic or pessimistic, utopian or dystopian.[18] Rousseau discerned in man a deep conflict between natural consciousness and social consciousness. Shunning compromise, he eloquently dramatizes this moral struggle, making what I have called conflict look like contradiction. Yet he is a very earnest thinker too, and so he boldly attempts in his three most ambitious works written at about the same time—*Emile, Julie: or The New Eloise,* and *The Social Contract*—to bridge contradiction.

The essential strategy, pursued somewhat differently in each of these works, is to show how natural man might live in a civil society by supplementing his given innocence with a learned virtue. "Virtue" is defined in *Emile* as "courage" and is needed "as the passions awake." For Rousseau knew (despite his woeful confusion of male and female with masculinity and femininity) that sexuality is the element of human nature most difficult to educate and that therefore a learned virtue must supplement a natural goodness if human beings in civilized life were to learn to guide their passions.

His teaching in regard to man's fear of death is in line with this. Anxiety about death is not present in a state of nature but develops monstrously in civil society. Rousseau wavers a little as to whether natural man doesn't know such fear at all or knows only so much as is consistent with his need for self-preservation. But the treatise's chief point in this regard is that Emile should be carefully exposed to the reality of death by his teachers precisely so that he will not be overly impressed by it and will continue to see death in the light of mere necessity when he enters the complex world of civilized life. Rousseau reasoned that this troublesome fear of death has been for the most part artificially produced, leading us to depend on priests, philosophers, and doctors, whose anxious, self-conscious teachings only heighten it. "By nature a man bears pain bravely and dies in peace. It is the doctors with their rules, the philosophers with their precepts, the priests with their exhortations, who debase the heart and make us afraid to die."[19]

As the Savoyard Priest is intoxicated by the word "nature," Julie, the heroine of *The New Eloise,* is intoxicated by "virtue." This epistolary novel describes a society, to be sure, but a small and ideal one, far from Paris in "a little town at the foot of the Alps" (not far from Geneva, one may suppose). Led by Julie, this small group has learned to transform sexual into moral passion, has learned both how to love (without jealousy) and how to die (without fear). The two lovers—Julie, wife and mother, and her former tutor, Saint-Preux—put virtue at risk by the strength of their passions, which gives some of their letters a Richardsonian heat, deriving in part from the psychological *regression* that accompanies their moral *progression*. (They tend to think of one another as young siblings or, more often, as mother and child.) But each has become able—especially Julie and especially after she suffers the accident that will lead to her death—not to choke this passion but to sublimate it. "Grand passions," she writes her partner in ardent virtue, "are usually crushed; rarely are they purified. But to forget what makes love dear in deference to respectability is the effort of conventionally virtuous people. That such lovers as we were can remain ardent as friends—that is the real triumph of virtue."[20] And this achievement will be capped by her exemplary death.

Conveyed in a long letter from her husband, Wolmar, to her lover, Saint-Preux, Rousseau's Julie establishes with great care the importance of her last hour. For her rationalist husband, despite his grief, it is unimportant to judge the moment itself, given the finality of death. For the pastor, who arrives as a Christian to instruct Julie but is at length instructed *by* her, the judgment on a completed life is God's, but for Julie such judgment is indistinguishably her own as well. Although as a human being she knows she cannot be free of fault, she knows also that her intentions were always pure and her actions always sincere, and so her clear conscience exempts her from any remorse or fear. She explains to the pastor the theological basis of this judgment: God is kind and just so he could not have asked from her more than he has given her. Thus, "La préparation à la mort est une bonne vie; je n'en connais point d'autre" (544). [The preparation for death is a life well-lived. I recognize no other.] Dying is merely an affair of nature and can be approached without fear. And the pastor concedes that her conscience will not deceive her and that her death, like her life, is beautiful.

Rousseau gives one more turn to this exemplary death by way of the posthumously delivered letter that Julie has written to Saint-Preux. It looks at first like a retreat from, but it is really an extension of, the sublimated ardor she had earlier endorsed as the bond between them: "Il faut renoncer à nos projets. Tout est changé, mon bon ami: souffrons ce changement sans murmure; il vient d'une main plus sage que nous" (564). [We must give up our plans. Everything is changed, my dear friend: let us endure this change without protest; it comes from a wiser hand than ours.] Death obviously requires the renunciation of the intimacy between them, but since God's wisdom and her own combine, this is really sublimation raised to a still higher level. Rousseau has quite remarkably fused the sorrow of human pathos and the triumph of divine will.

The concept of ideal virtue supporting the abstract argument of *The Social Contract* is similar in substance to that in *Julie*, despite the difference in tone. The treatise raises the question: How can the liberty and republicanism that Rousseau always valued be joined to the moral regulation required to withstand the corrupting influences of society? The answer, to put a complex argument as simply as possible, is that people in this ideal state have learned to identify their individual wills with the general will. As Arthur M. Meltzer neatly puts it, *The Social Contract* teaches not "the rule of some over others but all over each."[21] In the equally neat phrasing of Lester G. Crocker, it teaches that man's "true will . . . is that the general will shall rule."[22] The paradoxical idea that it turns on is that, as Rousseau puts it, man "shall be forced to be free."[23] The paradox is more or less resolved by the supposition that we give our consent to this force because we are willing to lose natural liberty in order to gain civil liberty. We have not so much compromised with our love of liberty as we have come to understand liberty in a higher sense. The underlying logic of *The Social Contract* is not so different, then, from that of *Julie* despite the obvious formal differences between the two works. In each case, the goal is to protect liberty by converting an individual into a social form of it.

Aspects of Rousseau's moral vision may seem to us conservative—his insistence on a kind and just Supreme Being (Voltaire and Diderot are evidently more subversive in this respect), his distance from practical political progress, and his distrust of imagination. Hence his profound influence on his Romantic successors, far greater than that of Diderot or Voltaire, requires a word of explanation.

Despite his distrust of the Romantics' sacred word "imagination" (suspect because he judged it to be a faculty fed by the "caprices" [artifices] and "pièges" [traps] of civilization), Rousseau's eloquent advocacy of individual feeling as the new moral center promoted the kind of personal spirituality that became a hallmark of Romanticism. His late book *Reveries of the Solitary Walker*, combining the stress on feeling with the charm and pathos of solitude, was especially influential in this regard. Similarly, his view of religious faith and the social contract, though not programmatically subversive, was radically original in locating the source of authority within the individual rather than within institutions, and this had the effect of widening the distance between individual and social authority. In particular, teaching us that our anxious fear of death was culturally produced had the curious effect of undermining civilized defenses against that fear erected by medicine, religion, and philosophy, thus leaving us more nakedly exposed to it. Whatever Rousseau's intention, his clearing of the ground led to the work of those pioneering writers of the Romantic period who formulated for the first time an existential view of death.

Opposing the Void

The Romantic Period

The epistemological shift from Enlightenment to Romanticism has been described by Isaiah Berlin as the greatest turning point in the history of thought. "During the entire span of the central tradition of Western thought, it had been assumed that all general questions [questions ranging from 'what are the best values' to 'does God exist'] were of the same logical type: they were questions of fact . . . answerable in the form of universal truth." He explains that the skeptic Hume and the atheist Holbach shared with G. E. Lessing, the very voice of the Enlightenment, the belief that the moral "goal was one for all men," however different the paths toward it. But when it began to be believed that truth was made rather than found, the notion of a universal standard of truth to be discovered either out there independent of our language about it or in an intrinsic human nature could no longer be maintained.[1]

Rousseau and Kant would have been dismayed by the shift from a universal standard of moral judgment (nature, conscience) to one that sanctioned the exploration of subjectivity and trusted in the truth of the imagination. Giving rein to imagination was something Rousseau warned against because it widened the gulf between our needs and desires. For the natural man abiding in us, death is not a harsh reality to be courageously faced but merely a natural necessity that we accept. We become fearful only when we forsake simplicity and allow ourselves, under the pressure of civilization, to become envious and competitive. For the leading Romantic writers, however, fear of death could not be explained, or explained away, in that manner. Rousseau's wise and good Creator had become too remote. Our "existence," in Byron's phrase, was now "sad and unallied." Without confidence in the consolatory promise of an afterlife, the Romantics found themselves staring into a void, although they learned various ways to oppose it.

The very words "life" and "death" take on new meaning in the Romantic period, as we see most clearly in the concentrated utterances of the lyric poets. The stanza of Wordsworth's "Ode: Intimations of Immortality" that precedes the final turn concludes by calling the poet's burden of despair "Heavy as frost and deep almost as life," where life, divested of "the visionary gleam," signifies a spiritual death. Shelley's title "The Triumph of Life" denotes the triumph of experience over imagination, a similar spiritual death. Coleridge in "The Rime of the Ancient Mariner" opposes mortal "Death" to "Life-in-Death," the latter yet another way of describing the death of the spirit. Keats in "Ode to a Nightingale" contrasts Death with a capital D, standing for the transcendent world of the nightingale's song (an "easeful Death" with which the poet is "half in love"), to a lowercase "death" signifying the ordinary world of mortality ("Thou wast not born for death, immortal bird"). Without imaginative enhancement—and it shouldn't be forgotten that the Romantics explored this impoverished state as well as its ideal opposite—death appears as the mere obverse of life, there being no other reality.

The exploration of such dangerous new material found literary expression that has seemed to some morbid. Although the once influential thesis put forward by scholars like Mario Praz (in *The Romantic Agony*) and Irving Babbit (in *Rousseau and Romanticism*) about the morbidity of Romanticism has largely been discredited, it still has some currency, indicated by Ariès's *Images of Man and Death*, which judged the visual art of the whole nineteenth century under the rubric of Romantic decadence. Such an indictment fails to understand that the seeming pathology of High Romanticism results from a bold and original inquiry into new imaginative territory. Seeking knowledge beyond bounds, confronting and finding words for fear of the unknown—such acts of mind may suggest morbidity, and they certainly entail emotional risk, but they may also be seen as proof of mental strength and courage, of psychological and moral resourcefulness. The poet-hero of the Romantic period undertakes to perform the work of the tragic hero in Shakespearean drama and (a morally upgraded version) of Satan in *Paradise Lost*. The Romantic Satan is usually dignified with the new name of Prometheus, as in Mary Shelley's *Frankenstein*, subtitled *The New Prometheus*, in Percy Shelley's *Prometheus Unbound*, whose prefatory note explicitly defends this replacement, and in Byron's poem "Prometheus." This is not mere bravado but a new awareness of life's abrupt end, of its existential character. Traditional religious guidance became for some only a bitter form of nostalgia. As Byron tartly remarked: "We are miserable enough in this life, without the absurdity of speculating upon another."[2]

The anxiety generated by breaking new imaginative ground, however, brought into play certain defensive strategies. One is the use of a new kind of comic irony in facing nothingness, by which courage and fear may be expressed simultaneously. In an episode from Jan Potocki's *The Manuscript Found in Saragossa*, for example, the narrator gives us a picture, touching and absurd at once, of his father who is preparing for suicide. Like Dr. Frankenstein, the father was drawn to the forbidden study of natural philosophy and tried accordingly to explain the natural world without reference to the glory and will of a Creator. But his brave antitheistic manuscript has attracted only rats, not booksellers. So, with appropriate ritual gestures, he gives a farewell speech in which he seeks to be loyal to his rebellious view. In dying, he will embrace nothingness: "Nothingness receive thy prey." But the boldness of the gesture is marred, first by the self-pity in his sour remark about rats and booksellers, and then by the doubts laced into his equivocal (and quite funny) prayer: "O God, if there is one, have pity on my soul if I have one."[3]

A second defensive maneuver is exemplified by the whole Gothic tradition extending from Horace Walpole to Ann Radcliffe, Charles Maturin, Edgar Allan Poe, and beyond. In contrast to the Promethean tradition that heroicizes the mind of the protagonist struggling with the idea of unallied existence (and its corollary, unredeemed death), writers in the Gothic tradition find excitement (sometimes of a sadomasochistic kind) in preternatural adventure. They manage, when successful, to convert the revulsion of horror into the excitement of terror.[4]

Although the most assured forms of afterlife consolation are discarded in this tradition, a compromise version of them is retained. In Radcliffe's *Mysteries of Udolpho* (1794), for example, the father of the heroine, despondent and near death, declares: "We are not enjoined to believe that disembodied spirits watch over the friends they have loved, but we may innocently hope it. It is a hope I will never resign. It will sweeten the bitter moment of death. Severe indeed would be the pangs of separation, if we believed them to be eternal." The passage expresses an inclination to believe in disembodied spirits, but in terms of hope and need rather than doctrine.[5] Another interesting example is Maturin's novel, *Melmoth the Wanderer* (1820), a story of selling one's soul to a demonic spirit for the questionable gain of extended life and extraordinary power. Maturin does not try to show, as Goethe does in *Faust*, that a diabolical alliance might ultimately lead to a redemptive wisdom. Rather, he is attracted to the uncanny aspect of such experience, to the excitement of terror. A clergyman, Maturin was careful to indicate that everyone to whom Melmoth tries to pass on his accursed gain refuses it in staunch Christian fashion, but his Christian moralism was no match, imaginatively, for the thrill provided by his demonic Gothicism.[6]

There is a residue of afterlife belief in Gothic fiction, but the best word to describe this belief is probably not supernatural but preternatural because it entails not so much another world as uncanny experience in this one. The interest lies in forbidden or alien thoughts rather than in a different order of reality. What is commonly called the marvelous in Gothic fiction is likely to be sparked by some kind of near-death experience rather than fantastic intrusion from beyond. Poe's stories, for example, exploit situations like premature burial, extraordinary survivorship from a natural disaster, willpower strong enough to bring the apparently dead back to life. In general, the Gothic tradition imagines dying itself as some sort of heightened experience, a theme that was refined in the work of more sophisticated writers of the nineteenth century like Whitman and Dickinson. Unlike the Promethean tradition contemporaneous with it, Gothicism does not reflectively explore the fear of death, but it at least entertains the idea of sheer nothingness, as writers before the eighteenth century really did not.

The boldest of the Romantic Private Prometheans is a writer outside the English tradition, Giacomo Leopardi, who quite deserves to be called an existentialist *avant la lettre*. Schooled by Lucretius as well as Rousseau and Locke, he denied belief in God or in any other spiritual power. For Leopardi, modern civilized man faced the nearly unbearable vision of *nulla* (empty existence as the sole reality) and therefore had to undergo the experience of *noia* (desire never able to find satisfaction in any earthly thing). And this turned into a desire for nothingness itself—a desire that, like all desire, is based on illusion, but is nonetheless sublime because it lifts man above reality. It is an embrace of the infinite. Here you have the essential elements of Romantic existentialism: recognition of the void, defiance of it, and the ability to make this very defiance look not only desperate but also heroic. No more successfully than Lucretius could Leopardi overcome the fear of death, but the energy of his recognition and of his reactive response make him a true modern Prometheus.[7]

I want to highlight in this chapter some dramatic poems and novels (*Manfred, Cain, Frankenstein,* and *Wuthering Heights*) that develop the elements of incipient existentialism more explicitly than lyrics do and thus

help provide an ampler context for the poems to be closely analyzed in subsequent chapters. But it is important to take notice first of certain
imaginings of death in this period that show us a subtler side of Romanticism, poems that try to find spiritual gain in the very consciousness of spiritual loss. These poems also oppose the void, but, because they do so in a
nonconfrontational way, their real contribution to the emergence of an existential viewpoint must be teased out a little.

Wordsworth in his great Ode is torn between the realistic need to acknowledge irrevocable loss and the idealistic need to resist this acknowledg-
ment because of "the indomitableness of the spirit within me" (in the phrasing of his introductory comment on the poem). The poet resolves the
conflict by discovering strength "In the soothing thoughts that spring / Out
of human suffering: / In the faith that looks through death, / In years that
bring the philosophic mind." The Christian religion was the traditional
source of a faith that looked "through death," but for this poet a "natural
supernaturalism" (to use the phrase made famous by Thomas Carlyle and
later by the critic M. H. Abrams) derives from the mind's working over its
"recollections of early childhood."

Consider another example from Wordsworth, "A Slumber Did My Spirit
Seal," one of the so-called Lucy poems:

> A slumber did my spirit seal,
>   I had no human fears:
> She seemed a thing that could not feel
>   The touch of earthly years.
>
> No motion has she now, no force;
>   She neither hears nor sees;
> Rolled round in earth's diurnal course,
>   With rocks, and stones, and trees.

With delicate ambiguity, this little elegy both denies and accepts the death of
a child with whom the speaker identifies himself. Motionless in death, she is
still part of the earth's ongoing motion, suggesting an animating connection
between man and nature that has not, or not yet, been broken. Geoffrey
Hartman observed, "nature, for Wordsworth, is not an 'object' but a presence and a power; a motion and a spirit."[8] Accordingly the speaker's expected grief is a kind of "slumber" beyond fear—or beyond "human fears,"
a puzzling phrase. Since there would seem to be no other kind, the poem
brings into play the subtle idea of a state of mind somewhere between grief

deniable because the connection with nature remains and grief undeniable because the connection is lost.

Another instance of Romantic death-of-self poetry that conveys religious feeling without reference to religion is the last part of Shelley's "Adonais." The poem is of course an elegy on the death of Keats, but in these incandescent latter stanzas the poet focuses attention on himself, his shattered hopes and residual idealism, his wish to die and the meaning of death. "The One" and "Eternity" stand for this idealism, whereas "the many" and the "dome of many-coloured glass" stand for the shattered hopes. Both, as stanza 52 tells us, will be trampled to fragments by Death. But the eloquently expressed wish to die that follows this realization is finely ambiguous. On the one hand, dying is fearful even though there is nothing any longer to live for: "Why linger, why turn back, why shrink my Heart?" It is pictured in the final stanza as a kind of drowning: "my spirit's bark is driven, / Far from the shore." On the other hand, in some vaguely spiritual way, it is associated with a realm of poetic immortality: "I am borne darkly, fearfully, afar; / Whilst, burning through the inmost veil of Heaven, / The soul of Adonais, like a star, / Beacons from the abode where the Eternal are." "Adonais" cannot fall back on the Christian imagery that supported "Lycidas," but its evident numinousness is still at some distance from a twentieth-century elegy on the death of a writer like W. H. Auden's "In Memory of W. B. Yeats," in which we read that "The words of a dead man / Are modified in the guts of the living."

I turn now to the Promethean subtradition in this period, which, like the Gothic subtradition, is a compromise with stark existentialism in that it grandly dramatizes the encounter with death. But it is a compromise of a more complex and serious kind. The protagonists of Byron, Mary Shelley, and Emily Brontë confront Death and Nothingness directly and with more awareness of what is at stake psychologically. They are bold in their will to face the unknown and to explore their unknown selves in doing so, even if, like Manfred, Cain, Frankenstein, and Heathcliff, their explorations are morally questionable.

The setting of Byron's *Manfred* (1817), a Castle in the Higher Alps, is evidently drawn from Gothic tradition, as is the time, Midnight. But the dramatic poem is concerned much less with special effects than with the mind of the protagonist, and specifically with his Promethean stance. A powerful mage, Manfred has sought "Conclusions most forbidden [in] the caves of Death" but to no avail.[9] The influence of Goethe's *Faust I* of 1808 is perceptible here (and *Manfred* in turn was to leave its mark on *Faust II*), but there is no equivalent in Byron's work to Faust's making a pact with the devil as dramatized in different ways by Marlowe and Goethe. Nor is there any counterpart in *Manfred* of the challenge that Goethe's Faust makes to Mephistopheles, asserting that he will renounce this life if he ever becomes satisfied by his achievements. We do, however, find in it a semblance of the Goethean theme of self-realization. The spirits summoned by Manfred are emanations of his mind, and his summoning them helps him to define himself and his situation, to explain his "mixed essence," after which they are dismissed. In the final phase of his life he will lean no more on superhuman aid.

Manfred has sinned grandly, openly violating society's taboo against incest. He claims to bear no grievance against society despite his inner desolation, and he bears his guilt proudly. But he feels guilt, and confronting this guilt and the despair associated with it is essential to his ultimate purpose, which is to die on his own terms, to preempt a traditionally divine prerogative by taking on himself the responsibility for passing a last judgment. Therefore the Spirit of Astarte, understood by Byron's readers as the representative of his half-sister and partner in the much-publicized incest of his own life, appears climactically. In this encounter, Manfred is much less defiant than in the preceding ones, more inclined to admit weakness. He is really seeking two quite different results from it. On the one hand, he wants to be able to confess his guilt ("I loved her, and destroyed her!") in the hope of finding "Forgetfulness . . . / Of that which is within me." On the other hand, he wants to accept his despair, to bear it proudly as part of his destined suffering.

Byron is thus seeking through Manfred to work out a view of the mixed essence of man, "half deity, half dust," a creature "alike unfit to sink or soar," too proud to sink, too degraded or guilt-ridden to soar. These contrary aspects are expressed in combination when Manfred says he will kneel to no one and nothing except to his own *desolation*. We are meant to be reminded of Milton's Satan, whose fate (as the Romantics saw it, though they were not unaware of his degradation in *Paradise Lost*) was to endure through strength of mind his own hell, for the mind is the Promethean spark, able, as one Spirit explains, to make "His torture tributary to his will." Manfred's speech to the Sun is reminiscent of Satan's famous curse upon the sun, and Byron particularly liked the speech.[10] It does effectively indicate the protagonist's determination not to regret the last hours of life because of an all-too-human need for love. He will stand, instead, on his own strength, and die alone.

The challenge for the poet, having deprived his hero of religious support, and having made him ready for death though not yet middle-aged (like Byron himself), is to avoid the kind of pathos that smacks of self-pity. In fact, the pathos in this dramatic poem generally remains controlled. Byron is careful not to have Astarte soften Manfred's guilt with sentiment, only to declare prophetically, "Tomorrow ends thy earthly ills." A somewhat different response to this challenge is required when Manfred deals with the two human presences he encounters, the Chamois Hunter and the Abbot, because they actively pity him. In these cases, the poet takes care not to make his hero's rejection of pity facile, and thus to make his defiance of fate seem unearned. Yes, Manfred intends to yield only to himself, seeking no mediation however well intended, but he is not contemptuous of either man, only formally respectful. His rebuff of the Abbot in particular, who represents the support of both religion and community, is positioned as a climax to the whole dramatic action. Byron apparently thought he had found just the right tone in Manfred's final, quiet spurning of the Abbot who would save his soul: "Old Man! 'tis not so difficult to die." Or so one supposes, for he was angered when the line was omitted from the first edition (possibly because it seemed contemptuous) and had it reinserted in subsequent editions.[11]

Burdened by guilt and supported by his own pride, Manfred has the courage to outface the dread of death, but death remains in the play something of an abstraction. And so *Cain*, a drama whose hero has committed not merely incest but *murder*, would seem to be the inevitable next step for a poet who wanted to pursue his consciousness of death to its limit. Lessing, in the spirit of Enlightenment, had declared in his investigation "Wie die Alten den Tod gebildet" [How the Old Picture Death]: "There is nothing terrible about being dead, and since dying is nothing more than a step toward being dead, neither is there anything terrible about dying."[12] But the Romantics wrote with the further knowledge that, at the imaginative, prerational level, there *was* some kind of dread to be reckoned with.

Manfred is a drama about confronting one's capacity to face death, and *Cain* is about enlarging the protagonist's consciousness so as to face one's capacity for murder as well, through an act of fratricide. It explores the meaning (or meaninglessness) of human life in general, not merely of one's own life, in view of the inevitable fact of death. After the fall of Adam and Eve, Byron's Cain knows in a general way that Death has been brought into the world, but he chafes at the thought. Why, for no fault of his own and because of a prohibition against knowledge of the truth that insults human dignity, should he and his kind be made to feel incomplete and insignificant? A product of the Romantic period, this Cain seeks full knowledge of his nature and destiny. He would have his consciousness be equal to his fate and is willing in his intellectual pride to bear the cost of such knowledge. The New Testament (Hebrews 11) had cited Abel as one of the heroes of faith. Byron would not have disputed this characterization as such but would have added that Abel's faith is a blind submission to authority and that a still more honorable though more difficult course would be to become a hero of consciousness.

Unlike Milton's Satan, Byron's Cain is not motivated by such petty and unworthy motives as envy or revenge but by a desire to know more, a high-minded but dangerous desire to seek knowledge traditionally regarded as forbidden. This makes him vulnerable to the skilled blandishments of "Lucifer," who, in the second of the three acts of *Cain*, conducts the hero on a cosmic journey and tempts him not with the promise of worldly glory but by rubbing in the idea that human life is a mere nothingness in the God-created scheme of things. Byron took pains to explain the originality of his protagonist's motivation in a letter to his publisher:

> Cain is a proud man; if Lucifer promised him kingdoms, etc., it would *elate* him: the object of the Demon is to *depress* him still further in his own estimation than he was before, by showing him infinite things and his own abasement, till he falls into the frame of mind that leads to the Catastrophe, from mere *internal* irritation, *not* premeditation, or envy of *Abel* (which would make him contemptible), but from the rage and fury against the inadequacy of his state to his conceptions, and which discharges itself rather against Life, and the Author of Life than the mere living.[13]

In working out this motivation in acts 1 and 3, which dramatize Cain's involvement with his sister-wife, Adah, and his brother, Abel, Byron does make some compromises with his conception, but they do not undermine it. They serve mainly to humanize Cain, to make him more attractive and less ruthless in his rebellious passion. In these acts, two aspects of his character are emphasized particularly. One is his love for Adah (and to a lesser extent for their child, Enoch), which deepens the pathos of his final banishment, for they will be his sole company. Although Byron wrote in his preface, "My present subject has nothing to do with the New Testament to which no reference can be made without anachronism," the play does in fact include a few allusions to Christian love. Adah, who would have Cain "choose love," says "atonement may one day redeem our race" and speaks of "another paradise" that may be regained. And Abel in dying asks God "to forgive [Cain]—he knew not what he did." The pathos of Cain's situation is the issue here, as the concluding action shows. When God's Angel finally condemns Cain to become a fugitive and a marked man, the hero feels the force of judgment to be almost more than he can bear. It is dramatized as a kind of second Fall completing the first.

The second compromise Byron makes is to suggest that, although Cain's irritation discharges itself *primarily* against Life and the Author of Life, it is directed also against his parents and his brother, so that it looks *not wholly unlike* resentment and revenge. Cain does blame Eve (more than Adam) for her all too consequential misjudgment and does scoff at his brother's "base humility." But the resentment of Abel is covered over pretty well by Cain's eloquent praise of him at the end of the drama. Byron even suppresses the envious motive attributed to Cain in Solomon Gessner's *Death of Abel*, which he had read. In Gessner's work, Cain dreamed that Abel's progeny would flourish at the expense of his own, prompting him to launch a preemptive strike, but Byron's Cain feels sorry for him precisely because his brother has died childless, leaving his own progeny to inherit the earth.

But it is nonetheless Cain the existential warrior, the warrior against Life, that comes across to us most forcefully, as in these strong lines:

> For what should I be grateful?
> For being dust, and groveling in the dust,
> Till I return to dust? If I am nothing—
> For nothing shall I be an hypocrite,
> And seem well-pleased with pain.

His crime is certainly not premeditated. Nor is he, in subtle Freudian fashion, a criminal from a sense of guilt, for he in no way feels the curse put upon him as his just fate. Rather he is a kind of Prometheus, recognizing, on behalf of mankind, his condemnation as the price of protesting against the fact that we are condemned not to understand the meaning of life. This is surely one of the reasons that Byron subtitled his play *A Mystery*. "Let me be taught the mystery of my being," Cain asks Lucifer in act 2, whereupon Lucifer plays up to this very desire, describing man's "immortal part" not as the soul but as *thought*.

As a Romantic hero of consciousness, Cain reminds us in part of Victor Frankenstein, with whom he shares a sense of horror for what he has learned and done, but he does not share Dr. Frankenstein's sense of guilt. He has been linked also to a tradition of Romantic outlaws running from Sade to Norman Mailer on the basis of discovering a heightened consciousness *through* criminal action, in accordance with Lucifer's suggestion, "It may be that death leads to the highest knowledge." But while this view seems partly justified by the absence in Cain of positive guilt, it ignores the very palpable horror that he does feel.

Byron's Cain also reminds us of Goethe's Faust, with whom he shares the sense that striving beyond bounds is not inherently evil, but Goethe's drama takes a different direction, finally linking intellectual with moral gain. Its Mephistopheles is not a tempter but an enabler, a prankster, and an ironist. Despite our use of the word "Faustian" to denote overreaching, Goethe, as Stuart Atkins pointed out, does not dramatize "the will to power or knowledge [but] the power of self-regeneration" through striving, suffering, and heroic acceptance of finitude. Gretchen too (whose story Goethe added to the Faust legend) is shown finally, when she is among the saints and angels, to have accepted responsibility for her actions. Although in large part a naïve victim of Faust, she is like him in gaining wisdom through action.[14] Goethe's opinions of Byron were copiously expressed in his conversations with Eckermann during the 1820s, yet they were of opposite kinds. On the one hand, he believed Byron to be the most extraordinary poetic talent of the age, the very personification of poetry. On the other, he was struck by the Englishman's recklessness and utter lack of restraint. These mixed traits explain why Byron exactly suited Goethe as the model for the figure of Euphorion in act 3 of *Faust II*.[15]

The theme of forbidden knowledge and the consequent confrontation with the idea of death as stubborn, existential fact is sounded again and memorably developed in Mary Shelley's *Frankenstein*, written shortly after *Manfred* and at the instigation of both Byron and Mary's husband. Since the work of writers who have come to think about death as unsupported by religious and social tradition is the concern of this chapter, we should remember that, as Shelley herself notes, the kernel of her inspiration was the "human endeavor to mock [that is, imitate] the stupendous mechanism of the Creator of the world."[16] But the tale boldly goes on to demonstrate that Frankenstein's sin is not so much his energetic pursuit of unhallowed natural philosophy as his reckless disregard for the human consequences of his creative act, an act that kills those who are innocent and dear to him. Although smitten with remorse, his is not the heroic remorse of Manfred or Cain. It is akin to that of Coleridge's Mariner, who, as a result of his moral carelessness, is burdened with incurable guilt and with an endless compulsion to tell his tale. This literary kinship is made clear through the character of Walton, the would-be Promethean, who functions like the Wedding Guest in Coleridge's poem.

Shelley does not fail to make good on her subtitle, *The Modern Prometheus*. Frankenstein tells Walton, with her implicit endorsement, that his fault was not yielding to creative and inventive enthusiasm but, rather, forgetting his duty to his species. What Prometheanism came to mean for the Romantics was not merely courage to defy the gods but, in Harold Bloom's words, "a heightened realization of the self," of its full capacity for creation and destruction, an increase in consciousness that necessarily involves an increase in despair.[17] This applies in the novel as much to the monster as to his maker.

It is of course the monster with his frustrated humanity rather than guilt-ridden Victor Frankenstein who steals the show. Backed up by Shelley's epigraph from *Paradise Lost*, he tells *his* creator: "I ought to be thy Adam, but I am rather the fallen angel, whom thou drivest from joy for no misdeed. Everywhere I see bliss, from which I alone am irrevocably excluded. I was benevolent and good; misery made me a fiend. Make me happy, and I shall again be virtuous."[18] In the most moving chapters of the novel, he recounts to Frankenstein his vain efforts to enter the human community, to be accepted and loved. But physically monstrous as he has been created or miscreated, he is met only with horror, and he turns against his maker not out of revenge but from a desperate desire to force Dr. Frankenstein to provide him with a proper mate. (His cry, "Make me happy and I shall again be virtuous," whether or not Shelley knew it, is a striking echo of one of Rousseau's best insights.) Under pressure, Frankenstein begins the task of creating a mate for the monster but soon abandons the project, smitten by a woefully belated scruple about doing yet more damage to his fellow human beings. And so the conclusion can only be the death of both antagonists. But the monster's has more dignity. His immolation on an impressive pyre is a chosen act and constitutes a protest against those who would sport cruelly with life. It is a death radically cut off from God and community, unhallowed and unmourned, but this is the pathos of tragic knowledge, not of sentimental nostalgia.

I have been describing literary confrontations with death in the Romantic period, a time when the vision of man's unallied existence first makes itself fully felt. The writers in question compromise with this vision, offsetting some of its inherent anxiety, by bringing into play two kinds of eloquence. In the Gothic tradition, the boundary between life and death is made mysterious and exciting. In the Promethean tradition, confrontation with nothingness is typically made to look heroic. The two traditions overlap to some extent, and there is no point in trying to separate them cleanly, but we may say they were jointly realized in *Wuthering Heights*, published in 1847. This is a date that takes us across into the Victorian age—a significant fact, for this novel allows us to see not only how the Romantic sensibility pressed against death at full strength but also how the sensibility of a more conservative age reined in this very tendency. This restraint does not of course lead Brontë back to a pre-existential view of death but prompts her to explore with originality the psychological and social ground of belief in an afterlife.

Wuthering Heights presses hard against the boundary beyond which extraordinary but natural effects become supernatural, the boundary beyond which the psychologically uncanny becomes ontologically problematic. Having earlier noticed the initials of the now dead Catherine I in the windowpane and having read her notebook, the visitor Lockwood sees her in a dream as a young waif lost on the moor and pleading to be let in. Then Heathcliff, hearing the guest Lockwood describe his dream, pleads with the ghostly Catherine to come in *this* time. It seems to us that each of the lovers is straining against the boundary of death to reach the other. A similarly striking instance of Brontë's pressing against naturalistic limits is the scene, narrated by Heathcliff to Nelly Dean, of his abortive exhumation of Catherine's grave some seventeen years after her death: "There was another sigh, close at my ear. I appeared to feel the warm breath of it displacing the sleet-laden wind. I knew no living thing in flesh and blood was by—but as certainly as you perceive the approach to some substantial body in the dark, though it cannot be discerned, so certainly I felt that Cathy was there, not under me, but on the earth." Heathcliff immediately links this experience to a memory of another incident occurring after Cathy's death. Having pummeled Hindley Earnshaw, he had hurried upstairs to his—and formerly her—room and "looked round impatiently—I felt her by me—I could *almost* see her, and yet I *could not*."[19]

Neither Catherine nor Heathcliff can be called an actual demon, but their attachment to each other is demonic in its intensity. This intensity leads her not so much to love him as to identify him with her very being and even with the very earth in which she will be buried; it leads him after her death to strain his will to the breaking point (his final physical collapse, the doctor implies, has this psychological basis) in order to unite himself with her dead body. Both desire a union in death that is not possible in life. (Cathy says of him, "I cannot live without my life, my soul.") The intensity of their wills is a novelistic given, in no way causally explained, although it nearly destroys the two family groups that make up the novel's civilized world. But it does not destroy them quite. Brontë's purpose is to maximize this intensity and then let it unwind so that the civilized world can be reconstituted, cleansed of what it cannot accommodate.

The novel again comes close to crossing the boundary of naturalistic possibility when, in a classic piece of Gothicism, Heathcliff bribes the sexton to open Catherine's grave and finds the beloved face almost unchanged after so many years: "it is hers yet." But this resistance to decay is explained by the quality of the earth in the yard outside the church where the dying Catherine explicitly and defiantly wished to be buried. "Not among the Lintons, mind, under the chapel-roof, but in the open air with a head-stone; and you [Edgar] may please yourself, whether you go to them, or come to me!" Her unconventional burial makes it possible for Heathcliff to rearrange her corpse in such a way that his own corpse will someday intertwine with hers, not her husband's. His anguish is thus pacified, the incident serving no further plot function.

The novel contains other Gothic trappings (the forbidding and remote dwelling, the surly and cruel host with his dangerous dogs and defiance of civilized behavior), but it contains little of the vulgar scariness we find in most Gothic tales. The emphasis falls rather on the psychologically regressive identification of self and other, on such a statement as Cathy's "I *am* Heathcliff—he's always, always in my mind—not as a pleasure, any more than I am always a pleasure to myself—but as my own being." Such love is less a love-*unto*-death than a love-*into*-death, a love for the earth that symbolizes life and death at once, both the wild freedom of the moor and the quiet peace of the grave. Brontë's prose narrative is reaching for a concentration of feeling that only poetry can really accommodate.

The love of Heathcliff and Cathy for one another reminds us, in fact, of Percy Shelley's desire for "one annihilation" with Emilia Viviani in *Epipsychidion* and reminds us also of two of Brontë's own strongest poems. One is "Remembrance," beginning with the lines: "Cold in the earth, and the deep snow piled above thee! / Far, far removed, cold in the dreary grave! / Have I forgot, my only Love, to love thee, / Served at last by Time's all-wearing wave?" The other is "No Coward Soul Is Mine," in which "God within my breast" is so totalizing an Other that it absorbs "Every Existence" in spite of cosmic annihilation and Death itself. This of course makes it an *anti*-existential poem, but it draws its strength from evoking the very void that its God absorbs:

Though earth and moon were gone,
And suns and universes ceased to be
And thou wert left alone
Every Existence would exist in thee.

There is not room for Death
Nor atom that his might could render void
Since thou art Being and Breath
And what thou art may never be destroyed.[20]

The stamp of Romantic tradition, then, is strong in *Wuthering Heights*, so much so that it almost seems to be the book's reason for being, but the ethos of a more restrained Victorian age makes itself felt too, and not casually, for gradually but steadily the narrative flushes out its lawlessness and violence. Mixing in a bit of the decorum inherited from her father, Edgar Linton, Catherine II has softened her mother's uncontainable wildness. Her spiritedness is lively and fearless, not desperate, and she becomes in turn the agent for lifting coarse Hareton Earnshaw out of his enslavement to Heathcliff and educating him to be a fit mate for herself. (The two Catherines are said to resemble one another only in their eyes.) In doing so, she will unite the two old families, the Earnshaws and the Lintons, and the two old estates, Wuthering Heights and Thrushcross Grange, which is the dearest wish of the novel's primary narrator and most trustworthy consciousness, Ellen Dean. But it takes some doing to purge away Heathcliff, whose unique single name suggests that he is as much an elemental force as a human being.

Found on the streets of Liverpool, Heathcliff has come from no definable place, and the dusky lad is brought by Mr. Earnshaw to his home and family without further explanation. Waif or not, he involves himself thoroughly with the two families, and, after being denied total possession of his beloved Catherine (by her will, by Edgar's will, and even by nature's will since she will die very soon after giving birth to Catherine II), he develops an elaborate and vengeful plan to dominate and control the others, indefinitely. It involves going off for years and returning a rich man, gaining ownership of Wuthering Heights from the vulnerable Hindley Earnshaw, marrying the infatuated Isabella Linton, and begetting a son who could become the legal vehicle (after being forcibly married to Catherine II) by which he can dispossess the others, enslaving young Hareton Earnshaw, and, finally, hastening the death of Hindley.[21] But the plan, though carried far, is by degrees frustrated and extinguished. Isabella dies. Young Linton Heathcliff, puny despite his virile father, lives just long enough to be forcibly married but dies before begetting a child. Catherine II, although made captive for a while by Heathcliff, maintains her spirit of independence and eventually ends his domination of Hareton. Finally, Heathcliff's own will to live fails, showing that the force dominating the action is defeated not only by circumstances but also by its own excess. The next generation will take nothing from Heathcliff. He comes from nowhere and leaves nothing behind.

Passion subdued, the end of the novel modulates into a quieter key. The last sentence is assigned to Lockwood: "I lingered round [the head-stones], under that benign sky . . . and wondered how any one could ever imagine unquiet slumbers for the sleepers in that quiet earth." Nelly Dean had just corrected Lockwood's use of the word "ghosts," saying she believed "the dead are at peace," which apparently inspires his just conclusion despite his previously partial understanding of things.

In its imagining of death and dying, the story certainly undergoes a shift from a Romantic to a Victorian ethos, a shift captured in Philippe Ariès's elegant comment: "everything that in an earlier novel would have been erotic, macabre, and diabolical becomes here passionate, moral, funereal."[22] But this should not be taken to mean that its morality becomes conventional or Christian. Nelly Dean is a good Christian, but Emily Brontë's personal God of Visions is an unconventional and fierce conception. It is Emily after all who created Heathcliff, a character who is subdued but not imaginatively erased, a character about whom her sympathetic sister Charlotte wondered "whether it is right or advisable to create beings" like that at all.[23]

The novel pivots on a balance between its regressive and progressive currents of feeling. It points not only backward to the Romantic tradition but ahead to the Victorian and early modern poets to be discussed in the next chapter. Both more anxious about conserving religious tradition and more pressured by the skepticism of their age than were their Romantic forbears, the latter group were obliged to invent new ways of imagining the end of life.

Modifying the Void

Mid-Nineteenth to Mid-Twentieth Century

For the five poets to be considered in this chapter, it is scarcely possible to revive the spirit of an age when the idea of death as a transit rather than an abrupt closure commanded broad communal support. The chief reason for the change of outlook was probably scientific development, especially in the areas of geology and biology. But these poets also resisted a narrowing of their religious horizon. They tried to salvage what they could from the consolations offered by a fractured tradition and to build new branches from the old trunk. Typically, their strategy was to avoid Christian doctrine as such, and, working with some favored element of the old myth, to build a new one, a personal myth bearing the signature of individual temperament. Tennyson and Dickinson fastened on the idea of immortality and invented new ways of thinking about the boundary between life and death. Housman and Yeats were spurred by their acute sense of loss to imagine suffering extended beyond life, and devised new versions of the old belief in purgatory. And Lawrence, responding both to the revaluation of death in the Romantic period and to later psychological science, reanimated the ancient myth of an underworld.

I have put to the side in this chapter not only antitheistic poets like Swinburne and James Thomson but also Christian poets like Christina Rossetti and Gerard Manley Hopkins, even though they may be as culturally embedded as those discussed. This requires a word of justification. Rossetti and Hopkins in particular wrote some strong poems about their anguished sense of emptiness. But they did not contribute to the shifting understanding of the end of life that I am delineating in these pages. Their abiding Christian faith in effect licensed the despair their poems express. Each of Hopkins's six sonnets of desolation (or "terrible sonnets," as they are sometimes called) was a kind of tormented prayer to one or another aspect of the Christian godhead, the existence of which is in no way denied even though its support is at the moment obscure. In perhaps the most powerful of these, "No worst, there is none," the poet cries out, "Comforter. Where, where is your comforting? / Mary, mother of us, where is your relief?"[1] Poetry of this kind continues to be written into the twentieth century, one notable example being the powerful "O dark, dark, dark" passage from T. S. Eliot's "East Coker," which plumbs the depths of desolation. But it concludes significantly by affirming that faith and love will turn darkness into light. And my next chapter will suggest that the frequency and influence of such anti-existentialist poems of despair have diminished.

In this chapter, then, I direct my attention to poets who were formally agnostic in the sense that they shied away from making confident claims of Christian faith. At the same time, they feared what Nietzsche their contemporary, in his parable about the death of God, also feared: "What were we doing when we unchained this earth from its sun? Whither is it moving now? . . . Are we not straying as if through an infinite nothing? Do we not feel the breath of empty space?"[2] Their imperative need as original poets was to modify this infinite nothing, to put it to creative use. Opposition to Death was too direct or too theatrical for their taste. A measure of the skepticism absorbed from the influence of new sciences was combined with their mythmaking. But their stance was still a reactive one.

The Nietzschean declaration that God is dead, wrote Richard Rorty, means that "human beings serve no higher purposes."[3] The five representative poets I discuss in this chapter create their own idea of a higher purpose, sharing (consciously or not) some of Nietzsche's dismay. Their poetic aim—to put the void to work—will be contrasted with that emerging in the mid-twentieth century, the philosophical spokesman for which I take to be Wittgenstein. For the later group of poets, the void has not become more knowable, but probing it has ceased to be thought of as imaginatively rewarding. Turning away from it, they focus less on death itself than on the end of life. In a sense, they have learned to take their existentialism for granted. Theirs are voices against the void in a more muted sense of "against," not voices of protest but of quiet and wry recognition.

Tennyson and Receding Death

I start with the quintessential Victorian poet, whose "belief in personal immortality was passionate"[4] and who worried not a little about religious faith destabilized by new developments in earth and life sciences. Although more conservative in taste than the Romantics, Tennyson had to wrestle at closer quarters with the mechanistic theory of nature, an idea that, as Alfred North Whitehead observed, the nineteenth century "could neither live with nor live without."[5] The Romantic poets were only beginning to feel this new pressure from the sciences. Their faith in the imagination overrode the mechanistic perspective, whereas for Tennyson the consoling conviction of personal immortality was directly threatened by it. He did not, however, want to fall back on orthodox Christian doctrine, and in this respect he was closer to poets of his age who worked *around* Christianity, like Brontë and Dickinson, than to those who worked *with* it, like Rossetti and Hopkins. Tennyson's poetic (though not extrapoetic) stance was characteristically tentative, equivocal, full of anxious interrogation. Is man's "tiny spark" anything more than "dust and ashes"? Are his aspirations anything more than "a murmur of gnats in the gloom"?[6]

Outside his poetry, Tennyson *was* often assertive about his Christian faith. In his one meeting with Darwin, he inquired challengingly, "Your theory of Evolution does not make against Christianity?"[7] He told his son Hallam he could hardly understand "how any great, imaginative man . . . can doubt of the Soul's continuous progress in the after-life."[8] Indeed he could grow vehement on this topic: "I would rather know that I was to be lost eternally than not know that the whole human race was to live eternally."[9] It may seem odd to describe a writer who so expresses himself as, in one critic's phrase, "a formal agnostic,"[10] but the poetry itself is far more uncertain. Although it uses the word "God," it prefers to hint at deity through images of veils, mists, clouds, and shadows. Basil Willey, describing the poet of *In Memoriam* with nice oxymorons, writes of the "poised uncertainty of the devoutly inclined agnostic mind."[11] The opening line—"Strong Son of God, immortal Love"—sounds confidently devout, to be sure, but the Prologue, written last, is "a conclusion more truly than an opening," and in the trial edition it was even printed above the title.[12] Moreover, immediately beyond its first line, the poem develops an agnostic thought: "We have but faith, we cannot know."

Because his adherence to Christianity did not reach beyond two general points—"there's a something that watches over us and our individuality endures"[13]—Tennyson did not worry much, as many Victorians did, about such matters as the inconsistency between the geological and biblical record. He found some degree of accord between science and religion (notably in the Epilogue to *In Memoriam*, which makes use of then recently published work like Herschel's *Natural Philosophy* and Chambers's *Vestiges of Cre-*

ation), trying to combine what he feared to be true and what he wanted to be true. The words he fastened on in this effort were "progress" and "evolution." Both imply forward movement and readily suggest moral improvement and spiritual aspiration as well as material advancement. The notion of inevitable political and social progress was, after all, in the air of Victorian England, and Tennyson was only one of many who chose to understand biological evolution as a doctrine of moral progression. But he did not pay close attention to the evidence. It was enough if it did not positively hinder his vision of unbounded futurity. When Darwin's theory specifically was in question, he would rise above it, remarking for example to William Allingham in 1863: "Darwinism, man from ape, would that really make any difference? This is nothing. Are we not all part of deity?"[14]

Tennyson always put man at the center of his thinking about evolution, and he did so in three ways. One was to speculate (in the spirit of Laplace's nebular hypothesis) that the cycle of biological life and of human life in particular was the last and greatest of a number of cosmic cycles of creation and destruction. Then there was moral evolution within an individual lifetime, the bestial element gradually worked out and the spiritual element becoming predominant. And finally he imagined a higher type of man arising at some future time, a type for which the dead but "living" Arthur Hallam provided the model. *In Memoriam*, the poem to Hallam, is his most elaborate poetic effort to think beyond death, even though Tennyson conceded to Knowles that the conclusion it reaches is "too hopeful."[15] (His less hopeful picture of death is well illustrated by the first segment of "The Passing of Arthur," written in 1869. But these lines are not very inventive, avowing little more than that "the eyes of men . . . have not power to see [death] as it is.") So I will start my examination of particular works with *In Memoriam* and then show how that poem's vision is extended and altered elsewhere in the canon.

The poem is widely admired for its palpable personal feeling. The main reason why it works through grief so slowly and so imperfectly is that the mourner insists on retaining the voice, touch, and image of his beloved friend. In the words of Clyde Ryals, it expresses "a refusal to say farewell to what [Tennyson] knows he has lost,"[16] and at its end even implies the restoration of physical contact, as if death could somehow be put aside. The poem is more than an elegy or even a series of elegies. It broods on and resists the apparent insignificance of life in general. Section 34, for example, asserts that "life shall live for ever more, / Else earth is darkness at the core, / And dust and ashes all that is." But this kind of either/or confidence cannot be sustained. The sections do not follow a straightforward logic. The thought weaves back and forth, following the drawn out, uneven process of mourning. At several points, Tennyson turns on what he has just said as if head and heart must each assert its truth in turn, or as if he hadn't put the case desperately enough. Christopher Ricks points out how the very *abba* rhyme scheme "contributes to the effect of the poem receding from its affirmations."[17]

The mood does become more hopeful toward the close. This is partly because grief gradually runs its course, allowing the poet to consider that writing his poem is no longer "half a sin" but a mode of healing. But it is also because he is finding a new way to think of Hallam's continuing life, which is by stressing the spiritual component of love and calling this a progressive "law" that leads matter beyond the body's material end. Law, thus fused with Love, looks beyond the boundary of death, and the poet can say: "I curse not Nature, no, nor Death; / For nothing is that errs from law" (#73). Repeatedly, the speaker has made a point of fusing Hallam's identity with his own ("I feel his being working in my own" [#85]), so that it is at last not difficult for him to think that their identities may merge in an afterlife: "I shall not lose thee tho' I die" (#130). This coming together is aided by the pattern of symbolic associations established between Hallam and Christ.[18] When, in the Epilogue, Tennyson writes that his friend "lives in God," it is not fanciful to suppose that he is imagining a reunion with Hallam, via Christ, "face to face," according to the Pauline promise echoed once more in "Crossing the Bar."

The God of the poem's final quatrain, however, is difficult to define: "That God, which ever lives and loves, / One God, one law, one element, / And one far-off divine event / To which the whole creation moves." The far-off event is surely not the last judgment, an aspect of Christian theology that held little interest for Tennyson. I think this conclusion is trying to express the ongoingness of life by way of love and law. Although it affirms an ultimate divine event, divinity has been associated throughout the poem with man's capacity for a love that looks beyond death. That is, the truth of immortality, of looking beyond death, is based on feeling rather than doctrine. Tennyson told Knowles, "If there be a god that has made this earth and put this hope and passion [for personal immortality] into us, it must foreshow the truth."[19]

In "The Higher Pantheism," written some seventeen years after the publication of *In Memoriam*, Tennyson extended his afterlife speculation in more logical terms. This poem attempts to be an argument as well as a vision of truth, and as argument it is undermined by excessive tentativeness. But it is worth brief attention before we go on to consider more successful imaginings of death's boundary—the dramatic monologues "Ulysses" and "Tithonus" and the lyrics "The Silent Voices" and "Crossing the Bar."

Pantheism as commonly understood is the belief that identifies God with the natural world. Tennyson wants to go beyond that commitment to naturalism but without saying, like an orthodox Christian, that God is transcendent, beyond nature. He needs mediating terms (like the Love and Law of *In Memoriam*) and finds them in the clustered substantives Vision-Soul-Dream, which in conceptual language add up to something like imaginative mind. This denotes a natural human faculty but also a faculty that extends from a material into a spiritual world. Robert C. Hill Jr. comments that Tennyson's version of pantheism "insists that the spirit is the only reality there is."[20] I'd prefer to say that Vision, Soul, and Dream are words that conveniently permit a transition from lower to higher uses of seeing and hearing. The merely natural eye or ear, bounded and unvisionary, sees and hears only so far, but the imaginative eye or ear opens a way to the divine spirit.

The poem is not a model of clarity, but it is not as confused as Swinburne's well-known parody "The Higher Pantheism in a Nutshell" makes it out to be. Two extenuating facts should be kept in mind. For one thing, it is attempting to work out as argument a hard-to-describe disposition "to doubt the real existence of a material world."[21] For another, the poem is full of interrogatives. The only noninterrogative couplets press into service the word "law" to suggest a progress that extends from matter to spirit, from human to divine. One could construct a paraphrase, running something like this: if visionary dream is possible and if it is true, we could call what we so imagine God. This sounds flat, no doubt, but it testifies to Tennyson's earnest desire to render an idea of divinity that is acceptable logically as well as experientially.

Tennyson's truest strength, however, is not to be found in the poetry of argument. It lies in the lyrical mode, and his fine dramatic monologues are nearer to lyric than to argument. In this form, contrary attitudes can be dramatized without worrying about logical contradictions. His most impressive experiment in conveying attitudinal contraries is, by common consent, "Ulysses," a poem that not only dramatizes contraries but also seems to reach into a deep and not wholly conscious layer of feeling.

Overtly, "Ulysses" speaks inspirationally for the spirit of ongoing adventure, of unresting travel, of heroic striving and seeking. But a recessed and opposite attitude is also conveyed. Goldwin Smith as early as 1855 commented: "[Ulysses] intends to roam, but stands forever, a listless melancholy figure on the shore." And Robert Langbaum much later spelled out a similar opinion: "Most characteristic of Tennyson is a certain life-weariness, a longing for rest through oblivion. . . . [This] is the emotional bias of his finest dramatic monologue, 'Ulysses'; though here the emotion is couched in the contrasting language of adventure, giving an added complexity of meaning to the poem."[22]

No other poem by Tennyson admits so directly that there is no personal immortality, that "Death closes all," that one can only sail "until I die." But for this very reason, perhaps, it is surpassingly effective in picturing this horizon as endlessly receding: "Yet all experience is an arch wherethro' / Gleams that untravelled world whose margin fades / For ever and for ever when I move." It is surely significant that Tennyson quite omits the *consequence* of Ulysses' "purpose / To sail beyond the sunset" as he found it in Cary's translation of Dante: namely, a soon appearing whirlwind that sinks the ship and drowns everyone. He turns a story of bold resolve resulting in extinction into a story of an endlessly open future! The longing for rest through oblivion is something we feel to be present in the poem. But this cannot be a longing for soul-destroying death. It must be a longing for oblivion only, for a melting of the self into the boundlessness of the sea. Certainly it reminds us of the account Tennyson gave his son of the "waking trance I have frequently had, quite up from boyhood, when the individuality itself seemed to dissolve and fade away into boundless being."[23]

Tennyson's deep partiality for this waking trance experience and for the corresponding image of an endlessly receding horizon inevitably brings to mind another dramatic monologue, "Tithonus." This poem again is making opposite claims. Overtly it tells us that death would be most welcome since endless life means endless old age. But what the speaker seems to be really seeking is not death but a dream of oblivion. The gorgeousness of the poem's rhetoric evokes feelingly a kind of suspended animation. Henry James admired its "poised and stationary" quality, and Christopher Ricks said of the poem: "we are in a world of impregnated silences."[24] "Here at the quiet limit of the world" suggests in context anything but an abrupt end of things, for the speaker, so placed, is "roaming like a dream / The ever-silent spaces of the East, / Far-folded mists, and gleaming halls of morn." Thus, by means of a dissolve-effect, death slides past, into the distance. Tennyson's fondness for the phrase "far, far away" is well known. It is usually taken to refer to what his Ancient Sage calls "The Passion of the Past." But it may refer as well to the future, not so much to suggest endless possibility as a mystic melting that eludes termination and extinction.

Finally, let us look at two lyrics written when the poet himself was actually not far from death, lyrics in which the themes we have been examining are expressed in a language that is calculatedly oblique but without the complexity of contrary emotion and contradictory logic that we find elsewhere. It is noteworthy that his wife set to music the first of these, "The Silent Voices," and that this poem and "Crossing the Bar" were both sung as anthems at Tennyson's funeral.

> When the dumb Hour, clothed in black,
> Brings the Dreams around my bed,
> Call me not so often back,
> Silent Voices of the dead,
> Toward the lowland ways behind me,
> And the sunlight that is gone!
> Forward to the starry track
> Glimmering on the heights beyond me
> On, and always on!

The three capitalized nouns of the opening quatrain all point to the cessation of forward movement. But the poem pivots on the phrase "Silent Voices." Although those voices call the speaker to "ways behind me," they also, in the last three lines of the poem, call the speaker forward. The imagery subtly circumvents the idea that this movement signifies a change from one realm of being to another. It is a change, rather, from "sunlight" to the "starry track," from "the lowlands" to "the heights," destinations that may but needn't be understood as otherworldly locations because they only glimmer "beyond me / On, and always on!" The propulsive "on," supported by a tripping trochaic meter, belongs equally to a here and a beyond, allowing the lyric to elude the question of a literal afterlife. The rhyming pattern supports this movement of the poem. The first four lines use an *abab* rhyme scheme, but the pattern then becomes looser. The last five lines contain one exact rhyme (a semantically contrastive "gone" in line 6 with "on" in line 9), a contrastive repetition ("behind me" of line 5 and "beyond me" of line 8), and one word ("track," part of the phrase "starry track") that recalls, with subtler contrast (*no* light versus *distant* light), the phrase "clothed in black" in the first line. In sum, the forward movement from day to night, from life to death, is fused with an upward movement, a movement from the lowlands to the heights. While we cannot miss the intimation of a heavenly goal, the imagery thus retains a formal agnosticism. The poem is a skillful compromise between religious tradition and a new secular ethos.[25]

We might observe, postscriptively as it were, that the compulsive but vague "on, and always on" is vulnerable to parody by a later age after onwardness had been largely emptied of spiritual significance. In Beckett's *Waiting for Godot*, the character of Pozzo comes on stage with a determined but meaningless "On," and leaves in the same way. But in a world where, as Estragon says, there is "no lack of void," the question of where Pozzo has come from and where he is going must remain an uninterpretable mystery.[26]

A compromise similar to the one in "The Silent Voices" is found again in "Crossing the Bar," a poem that features the traditional association of death with a sea voyage rather than with a starlit height.

Sunset and evening star,
    And one clear call for me!
And may there be no moaning of the bar,
    When I put out to sea,

But such a tide as moving seems asleep,
    Too full for sound and foam,
When that which drew from out the boundless deep
    Turns again home.

Twilight and evening bell,
    And after that the dark!
And may there be no sadness of farewell,
    When I embark;

For tho' from out our bourne of Time and Place
    The flood may bear me far,
I hope to see my Pilot face to face
    When I have crost the bar.

The movement in this poem from life to death is couched in an imagery that is seemingly neutral from a moral point of view, of daylight fading into evening and of a voyager putting out to sea. But the consolatory implication of a heavenly home is fairly clear. No word like "heavenly" appears in the poem, and the phrase "turns again home" in line 8 describes the natural turning of the tide out to "the boundless deep." Yet the unsounding tide that the speaker wishes for is one that "seems asleep," and, thus humanized, its outgoing movement to the deep is a turn toward a consolatory home. The two sentences that begin "And may there be" (lines 3 and 11) are equally subtle in the way they covertly admit a measure of consolation while overtly describing only a natural process. In the first, the "moaning of the bar" that the speaker wishes away is the sound of the ocean beating on a sand bar at the mouth of a harbor, but it suggests the presence of mourners who are not actually present. In the second, similarly, the speaker disavows any desire for "a sadness of farewell" but suggests such a desire by mentioning it at all. So, although God and community are formally absent in this poem, traces of these traditional sources of consolation, as well as a measure of the pathos they make possible, are present. In this connection, Ricks attentively observes that "the third line of each stanza, longer than the preceding line, swells into a release of feeling. But what saves this from self-indulgence . . . is the immediate curbing effect of the stanza's shortened concluding line, reining and subduing the feeling."[27]

Each half of the poem begins with a beautifully poised phrase: "Sunset and evening star" and, its parallel, "Twilight and evening bell." Around the little "and" in each case is grouped an opening spondee and a closing near-spondee (that is, three syllables, the middle of which is stressed almost as much as the other two). The alliteration of line 1 and the assonance of line 9 heighten the poised effect, as does the suggestion in "star" and then in "bell" of light and of sound subsiding to a fine, firm point. Then the images of light and sound are reversed with graceful intricacy in the line that follows each of these: a "clear call" follows "evening star"; "the dark" follows "evening bell."

The last stanza, featuring that ambiguous Pilot, has of course proved to be the most critically troublesome part of "Crossing the Bar." I do not think we need to fault the capitalized abstractions, Time and Place, for one could argue that they merely generalize the concrete images of the preceding stanzas. Nor is the archaic "bourne" with its Hamletian echo really a sticking point, for one could say that the poem plays *against* the third soliloquy's otherworldly "bourne" with an earthly meaning of the word.[28] But the Pilot is a genuine problem because its ambiguity does not function effectively. When Tennyson was made aware that pilots leave the boats they guide once the harbor-bar is passed, he explained awkwardly that this Pilot "has been on board all the while, but in the dark I have not seen him." He added, not very consistently, "[The Pilot] is that Divine and Unseen Who is always guiding us."[29] The hope of meeting face-to-face after crossing a boundary that is clearly symbolic of the boundary between life and death evokes inevitably, and with uncharacteristic definiteness, the presence of God. But the

Pilot problem aside, the final stanza of the lyric reads very gracefully, and the concluding line brings us back to the title, as if the poem itself is making a turn toward home.

One final word about the broader Victorian context of Tennyson's association of the sea and death, and here again Dickens provides a useful parallel. The dying mother of Florence Dombey is described as drifting "out upon the dark and unknown sea that rolls round all the world." The dying of Barkis in *David Copperfield* (whose acquiescence is marked by his repeating the phrase he used to propose marriage, "Barkis is willin'") is registered by Mr. Peggoty's words, "He is a going out with the tide" and the narrator's follow-up, "and it being low water, he went out with the tide." Dying in these instances is evidently a more sentimental matter than it is in "Crossing the Bar," but this is in large part due to the fact that a novel creates deathbed *scenes* involving mourners, whereas a lyric describes an individual and private mood, without dialogue or characters. The link that concerns us involves the way Dickens too, as a Victorian, employs inventive indirection and allusion to suggest religious consolation. A sea that "rolls round all the world" is not obviously a spiritual comfort, yet it could suggest an embrace. The coincidence of dying with the turning of the tide in both "Crossing the Bar" and *David Copperfield* is similarly oblique, holding out the possibility of, but not promising, the guidance of an unseen hand.

One might contrast these Victorian pictures to what we find in Shakespeare on the one hand and Wallace Stevens on the other. Falstaff's death in *Henry V* is also described (by the Hostess) as occurring "ev'n at the turning o' th' tide." But Shakespeare does not hesitate to joke pleasantly about the Hostess comparing Falstaff's parting to that "of any christom child" or about her ignorant mistaking of Arthur's for Abraham's bosom or about her endearingly awkward way of consoling the dying knight ("I hoped there was no need to trouble himself with [thoughts of God] yet"). In contrast, during the century after Tennyson's, we have Stevens describing the human world as "an island solitude, unsponsored, free, / Of that wide water, inescapable." This wide water refers only to our naked, mortal condition. Our solitude is unsponsored, unallied, surrounded by unresponsive void.

Dickinson and Awesome Death

Certain capitalized nouns with high Christian resonance—especially Immortality, Eternity, Heaven, and God—permeate Emily Dickinson's poetry, but their meaning is always guided by her independent imagination. "Religion," Charles Anderson observed, "could never be acceptable to her as convention and would have to be explored anew as a whole way of life."[30] Alfred Kazin, making a similar point, wrote that Dickinson "did not believe in 'God' and His mysteries so much as she possessed them for her own purposes."[31] Certainly she made use of the vocabulary provided by her Christian education. It could intensify a perception of pain: in one poem the speaker refers to herself as "The Queen of Calvary" (#348).[32] Or of pleasure: another concludes, "In the name of the Bee — / And of the Butterfly — And of the Breeze — Amen!" (#18). But most of the poems that refer to religion or religious belief are mocking.[33] The letters take a similar position. "I do not respect 'doctrines,'" Dickinson writes in one.[34] And in another: "They [her family] are religious—except me—and address an Eclipse every morning— whom they call 'Father'" (L404). In one letter, she explains her dissent: "The mysteries of human nature surpass the 'mysteries of redemption,' for the infinite we only suppose, while we see the finite" (L506). This skews to her own purpose a biblical verse: "It is given unto you to know the mysteries of the kingdom of heaven" (Matthew 13:11).

The poet's vision was rooted in intensity of feeling, feeling "engrossed to Absolute" (#629). The cardinal point to make, then, about those capitalized substantives and about a handful of other words used in a similarly absolute sense—Dawn, Noon, Sunset, Midnight, Birth, and, especially, Death—is that they denote not metaphysical entities but aspects of mind, of consciousness. "For Dickinson the artist, the denial or affirmation of another life was all hypothesis by contrast with the drama of consciousness."[35] This apt generalization can be readily illustrated:

> Heaven is so far of the Mind
> That were the Mind dissolved —
> The Site — of it — by Architect
> Could not again be proved —   (#370)

Again,

> The Brain is just the weight of God —
> For — Heft them — Pound for Pound—
> And they will differ — if they do —
> As Syllable from Sound —   (#632)

And, simply, "Consciousness is Noon" (#1056).

Dickinson takes advantage of the fact that the meanings of her favored nouns somewhat overlap, broadening the range of their connotations. Immortality is inseparable from the most potent and resonant of her intensities, Death, and, indeed, an early poem tells us that Death is nothing else "but our rapt attention / To Immortality" (#7). In "Because I could not stop for Death," Death and Immortality are carriage mates, and, by the end of the poem, the speaker's goal is termed "Eternity" as well, a useful word because it absolutizes time: "Forever is composed of Now / Tis not a different time" (#624). In this poetic universe, metaphors of time and place easily mix: "Behind Me — dips Eternity — / Before Me — Immortality — / Myself the Term Between" (#721).

The word "Heaven" in Dickinson's poetry allows interplay with the contrastive words "Earth" (or "Nature") and "Hell," but poetic pressure usually collapses the logic of antithesis. In some poems, Heaven is indistinguishable from the glories of nature. "'Nature' is what we see": thus, "Nature is Heaven" (#668). As she explained in a letter to Thomas Wentworth Higginson, "The 'Supernatural' is only the Natural, disclosed" (L424). In other poems, heaven is shown to be, by virtue of its very magnitude and resistance to imaginative grasp, much like hell or death. "My life closed twice before its close" (#1732) ends with this stanza:

> So huge, so hopeless to conceive
> As these [closings] that twice befell.
> Parting is all we know of heaven,
> And all we need of hell.

About this poem, the critic Helen McNeil commented, "Heaven and hell manifest themselves through the same effect: in practical terms—and these are the only terms the poem is considering—they are both hellish."[36] The same could be said of #71, which refers to "an ecstasy of parting / Denominated Death."

The word "God" affords the poet the particular advantage of making personal and even erotic the relation between the desiring soul and an Other that can be understood as Lover, as Master, or as Deity. A good example is the poem that begins with the phrase "Wild Nights" (#249) and ends: "Rowing in Eden — Ah, the Sea! / Might I but moor — Tonight — / In Thee!" This poem has struck a number of critics as erotic, and I agree that it is, but "Thee" could refer to God as well as to a man, and in fact was probably influenced by Brontë's "No Coward Soul Is Mine" (a favorite poem of Dickinson's, read at her funeral), which is an intense address to the "God within my breast."[37]

What above all links Dickinson's major nouns is that they describe the *limits* of consciousness, the utmost of what can be imagined of knowing and feeling, of pleasure and pain. Probably the most important statement Dickinson ever made about her art is the little sentence that occurs in one of her letters: "My business is Circumference" (L462). By this she meant that her propulsive poetic desire was to engross, to saturate with feeling, the furthest limit of consciousness. Circumference is thus "the ultimate of wheels" (#633), "the God of width" (#1231), "the Bride of Awe" (#1620). The "Grave" is defined in one poem (#649) as "Circumference without Relief / Or Estimate or End." The experience of reaching a ne plus ultra of knowing or feeling is one she ardently seeks to express. "Heaven" is "the interdicted land" that "I cannot reach" (#239). "The Distance / Between Ourselves and the Dead" is "Further than Guess can gallop / Further than Riddle ride" (#949).

One very fitting word that this Bride of Awe finds to express the emotion of standing at such a threshold is "Awe" itself, a word fusing exaltation and fear at the limit of consciousness. Awe may be induced by an ecstasy of either pleasure or pain, although pain tends to predominate, especially in the latter half of the poet's work. When she writes, "Pain — has an element of Blank" (#650), she means that, experientially, it is infinite, hence absolute. The natural history of feeling, one poem suggests, sequences "pleasure" first, then "excuse from pain," then the anodyne of sleep, and finally "the privilege to die" (#536). Despair is "the White Sustenance" (#640) on which the imagination of Emily Dickinson feeds. Even the ordinary disappointment of missing a visit from Higginson elicits this kind of remark: "the finest wish is the futile one" (L500).

Masochism is probably not the right word to describe this aspect of her poetic vision (though it is likely to occur to us) because Dickinson regularly turns pain into power, as in this example, "A nearness to Tremendousness / An Agony procures" (#963); or this, "I love the Cause that slew Me. / Often as I die / Its beloved Recognition / Holds a Sun on Me — " (#925). It is not a wish for death that we sense in Dickinson's poems so much as an excited, awed consciousness of the idea of death, that most compelling of facts: "The overtakelessness of those / Who have accomplished Death / Majestic is to me beyond / The majesties of Earth" (#1691). The neologism "overtake-lessness," stretching the English language, conveys the wonder of a poet who was always fascinated by the unbridgeable distance between the living and the dead.[38] "It grieves me," she wrote to one correspondent, "that you speak of Death with so much expectation. . . . Dying is a wild Night and a new Road" (L463).

Even though the speaker of these poems is sometimes positioned as look-ing back from a point beyond life, it is important to see that Dickinson in-sists from first to last on the finality of death and the unknowability of any afterlife. What lies beyond death is a "sky of which we don't know any-thing" (L362), a sea "Unvisited of Shores" (#695). "Death is final" (#1260), something "We do not know" (#698), and life is the "stir / That each can make but once" (#1307). "The bravest die / As ignorant of their resumption / As you or I" (#1497), for "The Things that never can come back" are "Childhood — some forms of Hope — the Dead" (#1515). Nonetheless, the phrase "formal agnosticism" that I have enlisted to describe Tennyson's vi-sion is somewhat less appropriate for Dickinson because intellectual doubt was for her always less important than the stunning experience of the last moment, "the éclat of Death" (#1307).

A direct comparison between Tennyson's and Dickinson's ways of con-fronting death may be illuminating at this point. Both poets struggled imaginatively against the finitude of death and were obsessed by the subject of immortality. But the Tennysonian strategy was to employ a mystic dis-solve of the boundary between life and death so that the boundary in effect recedes. Dickinson in contrast was awed by the hugeness of the moment of death. When in a letter she called Immortality "the Flood subject" (L454), she did not mean that it induced a dissolution of ego-boundaries but that it empowered her mind so that the very act of trying to imagine it constituted an ultimate emotional experience.

The Dickinsonian stance regarding ultimacy should also be contrasted to that of Emerson and the Orphic Romantic tradition associated with him. The Romantics sometimes saw God in nature, and Emerson conceived of poetic language as a way of revealing a transcendental beyond, a higher symbolic knowledge, but Dickinson always kept God (who was for her a sort of neighbor, regarded with friendly suspicion) firmly apart from the natural world. To the inspired poetic eye, she implies, nature might temporarily *substitute* for heaven, but it never *symbolizes* a world beyond.[39]

The stance Dickinson typically adopts, then, is more active than passive, more explicit than suggestive. In one poem that begins "Of Death I try to think like this" (#1558), she likens her thinking to reaching for a purple flower on the other side of a roaring brook that she and childhood playmates were determined to get even at the risk of doom. This liking for bold action, combined with a marked tendency to present her speakers as incongruously small, often gives the movement of her poems a thrusting or explosive qual-ity, a recoil and spring from center to circumference. Jane Donahue Eberwein has described well this characteristic movement of the verse, calling it a "strategy of limitation": "Emily Dickinson tended to exaggerate . . . limitations, appropriate them for herself, identify with them. It is as if she drew tightly in upon herself until the very energy of her contraction exploded her, like a poetic atomic bomb, toward the margins of the universe."[40] She wants the soul's recognition of an absolute like immortality to come across as a shock, like the "Flash," "Click," and "Suddenness" of lightning (#974).

Death is the most resonant of this poet's liminal absolutes. "What fascinated Dickinson about death," Kazin wrote, "was precisely its coming. This is finally all we know . . . and it is the knowing we cannot escape."[41] I would put the point just a little differently. Death commanded her imagination because of its incomparable power to stun us into awe. Death "drills his Welcome in" (#1260). It is "the White Exploit" (#922), "Costumeless Consciousness" (#1454), "the Hyphen of the Sea" (#1454), and generates still other brilliant metaphors.

The compression achieved by oxymoron and paradox is vital to the rhetorical success of many of these poems. Oxymoronic phrases abound: "Sovereign Anguish" (#167), "imperial affliction" (#258), "docile and omnipotent" (#585), "heft of Tunes" (#258), "Bolts of Melody" (#505), "sumptuous destitution" (#1382)—to cite but a few. The paradoxes, though necessarily statements, are almost as compressed. "The Zeroes — taught us — Phosphorus" is the enigmatic opening of one poem (#689). After one gains some familiarity with Dickinson's verbal world, one sees what is meant: nothingness or lack itself provides the igniting powder that propels mind toward the margin of consciousness. Other typical paradoxes are: "My basket held just firmaments" (#352); "The Truth must dazzle gradually" (#1129); "Elysium is as far as to / The very nearest Room" (#1760).

Consider one that is more elaborate but hardly more leisurely in style, the complex paradox embedded in the last stanza of the poem beginning "My Life had stood — a Loaded Gun" (#754):

> Though I than He — may longer live
> He longer must — than I —
> For I have but the power to kill,
> Without — the power to die —

Poetic immortality had been merely potential before the writing of this poem (the year is 1863, her *annus mirabilis*), but now it is actual and irrevocable. "He" is whoever will preserve the writer's poetic life after her physical death, and so "I" has a double identity. One "I" is the mortal Emily Dickinson who may or may not live longer than "He." But "He" must live longer because the immortal "I," who can use words that have the force of a "death warrant," must be saved from neglect.[42]

Sometimes a compressive effect is achieved merely with commas—"Wrecked, solitary, here" (#280). But Dickinson's poems can also be too elliptical. When a poem fails (and many do), it is never because it is too slack and diffuse but always because its emotional freight is not palpable enough, because it is notational rather than realized. Therefore it may be helpful to round out this essay with close commentary on two that are successful, "I heard a Fly buzz — when I died — " (#465) and "Because I could not stop for Death — " (#712). Neither has been neglected by critics, but the present context may provide additional insight.

> I heard a Fly buzz — when I died —
> The stillness in the Room
> Was like the Stillness in the Air —
> Between the Heaves of Storm —
>
> The Eyes around — had wrung them dry —
> And Breaths were gathering firm
> For that last Onset — when the King
> Be witnessed — in the Room —
>
> I willed my Keepsakes — Signed away
> What portion of me be
> Assignable — and then it was
> There interposed a Fly —
>
> With Blue — uncertain stumbling Buzz —
> Between the light — and me —
> And then the Windows failed — and then
> I could not see to see —

The speaker, necessarily, reports the moment of death retrospectively but concentrates our attention on that moment. All preparation for death, like the willing of keepsakes mentioned in the third stanza, has been completed, and the only thing that the dying person now attends to is the sound of stillness and buzz—a stillness big with expectation like that between "Heaves of storm" and a buzz that, in the absence of other sound, turns our attention to the insignificant fly.

The poem retains a trace of reference to a supportive community in synecdochies that indicate the presence of others at the bedside, "Eyes around" and "Breaths." But this way of referring to others completely de-personalizes them and does not even suggest mourning, although mourning is normally expressed by eyes and breath. In this case, the now dry eyes have completed their weeping and the breaths are "gathering firm." Everything and everyone in the room is concentrated on the moment of death, the moment when "the King / Be witnessed in the Room." Possibly the King denotes Christ, but I take it to be a word for Death, traditionally the King of Terrors (or, in this poet's vocabulary, the King of Awe).[43] Her debt to the Romantic tradition is suggested by the personification, yet her generalized Death is hardly a mythic figure and the speaker is not made heroic in confronting Him.

After the third stanza's narratively relaxed comment about the keepsakes, we return, via one of Dickinson's less casual dashes, to the fly that interposes itself between the light from the window and the eye of the dying person. Then we move directly to the climax of the poem. Three canceling actions, reported in the quickest possible succession, mark the precise moment of death. First, "the Windows failed," a mis-seeing or mis-interpretation; then, captured by the brilliant phrase "I could not see to see," the virtually simultaneous extinction of interpreting consciousness and visual perception. Or is it visual perception and interpreting consciousness?

The poem is in some sense a tour de force. But it resembles Dickinson's effort in many others to convey the enormity and acuteness of the experience of loss, death being the most dramatic and irrevocable form of loss that can be imagined. Like Tennyson, she has worked out a compromise between a religious and an agnostic view death, but her style of compromise is more deliberately equivocal, more cunning and ironic.

Some comment on one more poem will round out our picture of Dickinson's way of imagining the end of life.

> Because I could not stop for Death —
> He kindly stopped for me —
> The Carriage held but just Ourselves —
> And Immortality.
>
> We slowly drove — He knew no haste
> And I had put away
> My labor and my leisure too,
> For His Civility —
>
> We passed the School where Children strove
> At Recess — in the Ring —

We passed the Fields of Gazing Grain —
We passed the Setting Sun —

Or rather — He passed Us —
The Dews drew quivering and chill —
For only Gossamer, my Gown —
My Tippet — only Tulle —

We paused before a House that seemed
A Swelling of the Ground —
The Roof was scarcely visible —
The Cornice — in the Ground —

Since then — 'tis Centuries — and yet
Feels shorter than the Day
I first surmised the Horses' Heads
Were toward Eternity —

This poem is distinguished not only by bold condensation of meaning (mainly in the final stanza) but also by its unusually skillful use of pace and tone. It creates a little human drama that meets its readers on universal ground—no one, after all, is ready to stop for Death—and leads them on a carriage ride that seems rather pleasant though we more or less sense its ominous implication. The tone is sustained so gently that the sudden collapse of the time frame in the final stanza from an afterlife span that includes a carriage ride to the abrupt moment of realizing death (a moment necessarily *at* the end of this life) constitutes a grand effect, in which the seemingly mild word "surmised" is charged with an intensity comparable to what Keats achieved in the "wild surmise" of "On First Looking into Chapman's Homer."

Death (before His presence imperceptibly fades) is a kindly gentleman guiding a lady into a private carriage—a relatively private carriage, for there is a third party but one with the rather reassuring name of Immortality. The drive is relaxed, marked by civility. Although the speaker had to surrender from her previous life even her leisure, she is somehow still enjoying another form of leisure. The sights along the way are pleasant too—children at play, fields of grain, the sunset. We are not so lulled that we fail to understand that this is a symbolic sequence marking the course of a life now ended, yet nothing up to that point seems plainly threatening.

With the next stanza, however, a countermovement becomes evident. The speaker, with a slight jolt, is aware that time is now not what it was and that she is encountering no ordinary sunset. She is aware too of a chill and of being vulnerably clad, although the sexual aspect of this hint is softened by the fact that no other presence seems any longer to be about. With the next, penultimate stanza, the tone darkens perceptibly because the House, though not called a tomb, can hardly be anything else and in any case looks forbidding. But it remains for the deft final stanza to zoom us centuries forward, then zoom us back to a time *before* death, and clinch the experience of awed consciousness that Dickinson took pains to create. The rhetorical device she calls on is paradox: centuries are shorter than the day or even than a mere moment of that day when death was first surmised. We are now, as we *always were, toward* Eternity, but normally we scarcely think about it. The shock explodes from an innocent sounding verb, "surmised," in a clause that seems to promise only a continuation of the journey. The experience, as another poem describing death puts it, is "so appalling — it exhilarates" (#281). The conventional business of religion is to soften the fact of death. Dickinson would magnify the shock of it as far as her skill with words allowed.[44]

No poet has come closer to giving force to Kenneth Burke's statement that death cannot be conveyed directly but only by metaphor, for she aspires (and knows she aspires) in her imagining of the moment of death to be as literal as possible. What Dickinson gives us is more than honorable failure, for she finds the language, the eloquence, that raises a voice against the void by making use of it, making a sublime something out of an apparent nothing.

Housman: Punishment Ad Infinitum

Responding to the skepticism of their age as well as their own spiritual need, Tennyson and Dickinson sought in their verse to reconfigure the idea of immortality. In response to similar pressures, Housman and (more complexly) Yeats sought in theirs to recast the idea of a purgatorial afterlife. The mature work of these poets issued from a consciousness of emotional distress so encompassing that it came to be imagined as extending even beyond death. Since an end of suffering was not foreseeable, they thought of their punishment as arising not only from their own minds but also from a world beyond. Many of Housman's poems dramatize a belief of this kind and make a notable contribution to the modern imagining of the end of life. Yeats is drawn to a more dynamic conception of a purgatorial afterlife in a dozen or so visionary poems that stand beside his other end-of-life poems composed in an elegiac spirit.

Randall Jarrell, with a touch of mockery, located in Housman's work two principal and not quite consistent pessimistic themes, each intended to shock us: (1) death is better than life; (2) nothing is better than anything.[45] This is too shrewd an observation to be ignored, and I will put it to use by arguing that Housman's verse acquires its most authentic pessimism by breathing life into these very themes and smoothing out the inconsistency between them.

Without doubt the pessimism of some of Housman's poems is facile, making them vulnerable to parody, for example those suggesting that no mitigation is possible for the usual disappointments of life (like a broken heart at age twenty-two) or that every friend is likely to prove disloyal or that every lad in the future will prove luckless in love. Jarrell comments wryly that the thought of any mitigation of suffering "would merely have added to his gloom."[46] But Housman often enough develops a poem beyond the reach of parody. "To an Athlete Dying Young" comes close to sounding cynical but is rescued through specific dramatization.[47] The poem's young man is not an everyman but an athlete, one of a small group for whom early glory notoriously fades quickly, and the poem retains imagery appropriate to an athlete without trying to make him a mere emblem of a depressing human condition. Its success is clinched in the final stanza, where the image of garlanded curls, enriched by association with the image of a girl's transient beauty, is shown to us in death undecayed (in that it has escaped the familiar fate of aging):

And round that early-laurelled head
Will flock to gaze the strengthless dead,
And find unwithered on its curls
The garland briefer than a girl's.

The stanza is reminiscent of ancient Greek epitaphs, partly because of the word "strengthless," an important notion in the Greek imagination of death (as Housman the classical scholar doubtless knew), suggesting the life of the soul without that of the body. So the poem is not quite saying "death is better than life" or "nothing is better than anything" but rather something much less facile if not less pessimistic, which I would paraphrase as follows: death may appear as an ironic blessing, but, imaginatively, life and death are continuous, pieces of one overarching ill.

We find this continuity illustrated again in a poem infused with an effective macabre humor (A Shropshire Lad, XII), such humor being another device that rescues pessimism from cynicism. The poem tells us that the "heats of hate and lust" are forgotten in death ("the nation that is not"), but it concludes with this uncanny stanza:

> Lovers lying two and two
> Ask not whom they sleep beside,
> And the bridegroom all night through
> Never turns him to the bride.

Once more it is the picture of life *in* death, not of life triumphed over or erased by death, that makes the poem successful.

In working with this trope, Housman learned to *make use* of Christianity, spinning it to effective ironic purpose. "The Immortal Part" is an excellent example. Man does indeed have an immortal part, but it is not the soul as piously believed. As any grave plainly reveals, it is the bone, the skeleton, that traditional image of horror, an irony that the poet manages to make eloquent. The "fire of sense" and "smoke of thought" must vanish, "And leave with ancient night alone / The stedfast [*sic*] and enduring bone." A more subtle and impressive (because more serious) example of putting Christianity to use is a late poem specifically entitled "For My Funeral." It resembles a Christian poem, invoking a seemingly benevolent deity who sends abroad his children "And then dost call them home." But the speaker's gratitude is based on the fact that the God who made him "wilt cast [him] forth no more"—into the misery of existence. The God this poem invokes "wilt shelter [his creatures] from sunshine / In thine eternal shade." Shelter *from* sunshine? This makes the light of life a curse and the shade of death an ironic blessing in that it cannot protect us from the painful memory of existence.

Housman's pessimistic eloquence is strongest, I think, in those poems where his speaker actively identifies with fate itself, with a universal dark grandeur that minimizes any sense of a boundary between life and death, as in poems that find language like this: "The troubles of our proud and angry dust / Are from eternity and shall not fail."[48] In *Last Poems*, XII, "the laws of God" and "the laws of Man," which one normally separates, are equally grand and oppressive forces. Thus a couplet like "A stranger and afraid / In a world I never made" is not self-pitying because its viewpoint is so comprehensive. One of Housman's best poems in this vein is the often anthologized "On Wenlock Edge the wood's in trouble." With a propulsive rhythm suggesting an inexorable force, the poem parallels a powerful gale of the present day with those that blew long ago in Roman Britain and concludes with an extrapolation into future time, the logic of which the reader must complete.

"To-day the Roman and his trouble / Are ashes under Uricon." So where is the ancient Roman's modern counterpart, and where are his troubles? The poem does not say, but in supplying the inevitable answer to these questions we are not encouraged to contrast troubles and *peace* but troubles and *ashes*, hardly a promise of comfort in the grave. The poem only *seems* to say that death is better than life, rising above cynicism by virtue of its comprehensive pessimism and its heightened language.

Poems of this kind may achieve a certain depth as well, and that happens when Housman acknowledges his individual sense of frustration—involving inevitably some allusion to his inhibited homosexuality—and folds that into the general indictment of life:

Others, I am not the first,
Have willed more mischief than they durst:
If in the breathless night I too
Shiver now, 'tis nothing new.

More than I, if truth were told,
Have stood and sweated hot and cold,
And through their reins in ice and fire
Fear contended with desire.

Agued once like me were they,
But I like them shall win my way
Lastly to the bed of mould
Where there's neither heat nor cold.

But from my grave across my brow
Plays no wind of healing now,
And fire and ice within me fight
Beneath the suffocating night.[49]

The poem, in part, looks forward to the peace of death following the fitful fever of life and hence appears to offer too weak a stimulus for rhetorical energy. But this thought is embedded in the *penultimate* stanza, and the final one turns again (and peremptorily) to the present tense and the present unhealable trouble, the suffocating night of existence. It is not the thought of an eventual release from punishment that lingers in the reader's mind but the thought of punishment extended into an indefinite future. It is hard finally to distinguish the darkness implied by "the bed of mould" from the explicit "night" of the ongoing present situation. In fact, the word "grave" in the first line of the last stanza looks to have been imported from the preceding stanza in order to darken the current situation.

There is one more searching Housman poem that I want to discuss in this little essay about his contribution to the modern imagining of the end of life. It is slightly regarded, probably because on the face of it the first two stanzas are weak, much weaker than the third and last. But I am convinced that this is deliberate, that the poet intended to create a sudden change in the level of poetic energy in order to dramatize the *process* by which a deeply authentic pessimism *breaks through* an apparent effort to suppress it and express a merely conventional wish to make the best of life:

> How clear, how lovely bright,
> How beautiful to sight
>   Those beams of morning play;
> How heaven laughs with glee
> When, like a bird set free,
> Up from the eastern sea
>   Soars the delightful day.
>
> To-day I shall be strong,
> No more shall yield to wrong,
>   Shall squander life no more;
> Days lost, I know not how,
> I shall retrieve them now;
> Now I shall keep the vow
>   I never kept before.
>
>   * * * * * *
>
> Ensanguining the skies
> How heavily it dies
>   Into the west away;
> Past touch and sight and sound
> Not further to be found
> How hopeless underground
>   Falls the remorseful day.[50]

The three stanzas align the moods of hope, determination, and remorse with morning, midday, and evening, but the smoothness of this progression is peculiarly undermined by the fact that the first two stanzas (unlike the third) are beset throughout by clichés of phrase, rhyme, and rhythm. So striking is this difference that we can't help wondering if Housman is seeking to create and maximize an ironic contrast between expectation and fulfillment. My conviction that he is indeed doing so depends in part (though only in part) on the presence of those curious asterisks. They appear in the first edition of *More Poems*, published in 1936, the year of Housman's death, and edited by his brother Laurence. In the *Collected Poems* of 1965 they no longer appear, most likely because their purpose seemed unclear to a new editor.[51]

In any case, the poem suddenly and unquestionably comes alive with the word "Ensanguining." It is its only unusual word as well as the longest, and one cannot read the poem without giving the word—particularly its second syllable containing the root meaning of "blood"—a heightened stress. The rest of the stanza also has a verbal strength quite absent earlier. Compare the banal inversions of "Days lost, I know not how" in the second stanza to the simple but eerily strong inversion of "dies / Into the west away" of the third. Compare the weak attempts at sustained rhythm in the last four lines of the first and second stanzas with the effectively cumulative thrust of the last four in the third, a contrast sharpened by the difference between the excessively simple vowel rhymes (glee/free/sea; how/now/vow) and the consonantally framed rhymes (sound/found/underground) of the last. And compare finally the parallel phrasing of "Soars the delightful day" (ending the first stanza) and "Falls the remorseful day" (ending the last). "Soars" and "Falls" may be evenly matched rhetorically speaking, but "delightful day" is mere cliché, whereas "remorseful day" is not. It is people who experience remorse, but here the emotion is projected onto the natural world, onto "day," which is then imagined as reaching beyond life into nothingness, a state defined by the absence of touch, sight, and sound. The dangling modifier "hopeless" is oddly effective in this connection. *What* is "hopeless underground"—the stated noun "day," the unstated pronoun "I," or, as seems most logical, the whole human and natural world?

The poem's deployment of the word "remorseful" is crucial to its success. The sense does not waver between "death is better than life" and "nothing is better than anything" but lifts both themes to a higher plane, a plane on which the acute emotion of remorse achieves a life of its own that extends into an indefinite future. But the speaker is not exactly denying that his emotion arises from within. We perceive this source in the two personal stanzas where it concerns his failure to maintain confidence in what is said in them, and then the emotion flows out, bloodily, above and below, into a purgatorial realm where no end is in sight. Since no escape is suggested, the word "hell" might seem more appropriate, but the kind of punishment to be

endured is no different from what we experience here. Housman's purgatory is a place where remorse and hopelessness, like life and death, are prac-
tically indistinguishable. And his pessimism is most authentic when it is
most comprehensive, when life and death together are pictured as a uni-
form, indefinitely prolonged punishment:

> To stand up straight and tread the turning mill
> To lie flat and know nothing and be still
> Are the two trades of man and which is worse
> I know not, but I know that both are ill.[52]

Yeats's Myth of Purgatory

The poem by Yeats that best introduces his myth of purgatory is "The Cold
Heaven," first published[53] in 1912:

> SUDDENLY I saw the cold and rook-delighting heaven
> That seemed as though ice burned and was but the more ice,
> And thereupon imagination and heart were driven
> So wild that every casual thought of that and this
> Vanished, and left but memories, that should be out of season
> With the hot blood of youth, of love crossed long ago;
> And I took all the blame out of all sense and reason,
> Until I cried and trembled and rocked to and fro,
> Riddled with light. Ah! when the ghost begins to quicken,
> Confusion of the death-bed over, is it sent
> Out naked on the roads, as the books say, and stricken
> By the injustice of the skies for punishment?

"The Cold Heaven" is similar to the poem by Housman just analyzed in
that it too pictures punishment meted out by an impersonal sky. (A heaven
of burning ice is more visionary but no more human an agent than an
ensanguined sky.) It is a punishment that the speaker in some fashion con-
nects with his own emotions but of which he cannot see any end. In
Housman's poem, day falls with the authority of a final judgment. Yeats's
poem ends with a question that shifts the emphasis from the finality of fate
to the speaker's baffled attempt to understand it.

In Housman's poem, we noticed further that the carefully placed word
"remorseful" links human agency to an impersonal fate. If it suggests a failure of will on the speaker's part, the cause of that failure is so sketchily

indicated as to discourage analysis. In Yeats's more complex and self-confrontational poem, the word "remorse" does not appear although it hovers in the background. More exactly, it seems to be canceled in the background. If "I took all the blame out of all sense and reason" for "love crossed long ago," the word "remorse," which the interpreter might well bring to mind, is not quite the right word. But the word regret is not quite right either. The speaker is "riddled" in the sense of being both baffled and assaulted by the memories of crossed love. From its first word, the capitalized "SUDDENLY," and sustained by its rhythm, diction, and imagery, the poem offers itself to us as the account of an imperative experience whose power, not merely whose nature, must be understood. The tone relaxes a little with the half playful allusion to the folk myth of The Wild Hunt.[54] But this only intensifies the speaker's final sense that he is nakedly exposed, stricken by an obscure injustice.

Yet "The Cold Heaven" is truly self-confrontational. The poet makes his complicated relationship with Maud Gonne a matter that demands understanding, from himself and from us. We know that the actual relationship reached back from 1912, when the poem was probably written, to 1889, when the two met, and that this span of time included rebuffed proposals of marriage, affairs on either side (on hers resulting in two children), her marriage to Major John MacBride (who is later described later in "Easter 1916" as "a drunken, vainglorious lout" redeemed by heroic action), and a night of sexual intimacy after which Gonne requested that their relationship become only spiritual. The biographical record (continuing up to and well beyond the writing of the poem) makes sufficiently clear that each party for different reasons both needed and backed away from the other.[55] It supports the poem's statement that "I took all the blame out of all sense and reason," yet supports the broader inference that, while the poet's imagination is (in a helpful gloss by Harold Bloom) "uneasily allied to the heart's defeat,"[56] it requires also an ideal form, gendered female, and that Gonne continues to embody that form. As John Harwood smartly sums up the matter, "Maud Gonne did not overpower [Yeats's] imagination; his imagination overpowered Maud Gonne."[57] One can't help being struck by the fact that, when she was about to marry MacBride, Yeats urged her "to remain the inviolate self he had so often celebrated,"[58] although by that time she already had children by another man.

We gain some insight into the poetic deployment of this material if we move back to "The Folly of Being Comforted," written a few years before "The Cold Heaven." It is dialogic in structure, consisting of two sections, a statement and a response. The statement offers comfort from a reasonable friend who says in effect: since your love is no longer the beauty she once was, it would be wise to reduce your emotional investment in her. The response, assigned to the heart, then sweeps away this advice, insisting that love's ideal form still lives, and would be apparent in the mere turn of the beloved's aging body. So the speaker *cannot* be comforted. Or perhaps he *will not* be, for there is ambiguity here. The heart's response is a bit overweening, after all. It does not say, "I should do as you advise but I love her too much." It seems to say, rather, "I won't do as you say because my art requires an ideal woman."

Another poem written between "The Folly of Being Comforted" and "The Cold Heaven," "No Second Troy," devises yet a different way (and a way on which the poet will build) of seeing Gonne in a double light. It makes clear that she has become an angry political activist, contrary to Yeats's aesthetic preference, but the speaker heroicizes this image of her by linking it with Helen of Troy, and then identifies himself with this idealization. Given her great beauty and pride and given the unheroic age in which she lives, how (asks the poem) could so noble a spirit *not* be angry?

Is there any way, then, for the poet to imagine satisfactorily a recovery of his loss and thus an end to the punishing sense of unfulfillment indicated in "The Cold Heaven"? Basically what Yeats set out to do in the strong poems that eventually grew out of that one is develop the conception of a purgatorial afterlife, a time during which the soul can purify itself of conflict and complexity. "No Second Troy" suggests the primary tactic to be employed in this enterprise, which is to discover in frustration and loss itself the very source of strength and joy. His reading of Nietzsche a few years earlier, whom he described in a letter to Lady Gregory as "that strong enchanter,"[59] was instrumental in this achievement, for it was Nietzsche who taught him that the realization of void could stimulate tragic joy and thereby self-transformation. Denis Donoghue writes persuasively of Yeats's debt to Nietzsche, observing that the poet learned from the philosopher not only to think of consciousness in terms of conflicting energies but also how to spur change between contrary states of mind and retain the tension between them.[60]

Yeats must have also been encouraged by Nietzsche to understand that the way to displace Christian belief was not with mere skepticism but with rival belief. Although always uncomfortable with traditional Christian ideas about an afterlife, he was fascinated by "the dead"—not so much by death as by "the dead," an idea that seemed to offer the chance to shed one's obsessions in a purgatorial extension of life. Perhaps he seized on Purgatory rather than Heaven or Hell because, as René de Chateaubriand had written in *The Genius of Christianity*, "Purgatory surpasses heaven and hell in poetry, in that it offers a future which the other two lack."[61] Yeats's interest in the *Upanishads* doubtless played a part here too—especially the notion of impurity being purged away through a series of rebirths.[62]

I will not in this short essay attempt to trace this conception through the intricacies of *A Vision*, but we can understand it better by attending to a handful of poems that make crucial use of that work. The first clear formulation of the new idea occurs in the essay "Per Amica Silentia Lunae" (1917) and is epitomized in one famous sentence: "I shall find the dark grow luminous, the void fruitful when I understand I have nothing, that the ringers of the towers have appointed for the hymen of the soul a passing bell."[63] Thus he who had been riddled with a keen sense of loss, hard to explain as either remorse or regret, would make *having nothing* a luminous and fructifying idea that aligns "hymen" with "passing bell," the perpetual virginity of the soul with death. This replaces the void understood as a mere cessation of consciousness with Nietzsche's generative void. Yeats finds in the idea of void a creative opportunity, a stimulus to his imagination.

Although the connection is not easy to analyze, I believe that the key link for him between the dead and poetry was sex. He told Olivia Shakespear, "only two topics can be of the least interest to a serious & studious mind—sex & the dead."[64] He needed to believe in his dead but not because he cared about the doctrine of the afterlife as such. Rather, he sought to verify an afterlife because the idea of recovering some lost object of desire at some future time aroused a sexual energy that in turn aroused poetically resonant rhythms and images.

I would describe certain major poems (including "Sailing to Byzantium," "Byzantium," "Dialogue of Self and Soul," and "Among School Children") as brilliant efforts to achieve an ecstatic override of the disturbing question set forth at the end of "The Cold Heaven." Let us look at these versions of Yeats's purgatorial myth and finally at the short play called *Purgatory*, which takes the problem introduced by "The Cold Heaven" a step further before ending in a final impasse.

"Sailing to Byzantium" opens with the poet's recoil from the prolific world of sensual experience, and thereupon, in marvelously compact rhetoric, the excited identification of an aging body's still ardent soul with the unaging monuments of art. The speaker, finding a brilliant phrase that combines skepticism and vision, hopes thus to be gathered into "the artifice of eternity." The poem partly humanizes the transformation from sensual life to impersonal art by invoking as intermediary not an artifact itself but "sages standing in God's holy fire" *as in* an artifact. In the final stanza, this change of state is imagined as accomplished, and the speaker is "out of nature"; his bodily form has become only a timeless representation that mimes the temporal actions spelled out in the opening stanza. But as some critics have observed (starting with T. Sturge Moore, who wondered about birds "out of nature"), that final stanza, despite its hypnotic language, is less than satisfying logically, for in it we lose contact with the world of experience and are contained entirely within the world of eternity.[65] Comparison is sometimes made between the endings of "Sailing to Byzantium" and Keats's "Ode on a Grecian Urn," and the comparison does not favor Yeats. In the ode, immersion in a work of art is shown more credibly as an inevitably transient experience, validated while it fades.

"Byzantium," though more hieratic in its imagery and thus less accessible than "Sailing to Byzantium," avoids this particular difficulty. Its imagery becomes more intelligible when glossed with reference to *A Vision*, but, even without that assistance, what is happening in the poem is fairly clear. A vision of perfection symbolized by a starlit or moonlit night is purging away the conflicts of experience associated with daylight ("the fury and the mire of human veins"), and this process of purification is sustained right through to an ecstatic conclusion. Unlike "Sailing to Byzantium," this poem does not end with a picture of passive, rapt contemplation but with a picture of intense mental activity, with the rapturous work of imagination, inevitably time-bound even if the imagery of its final line suggests symbolic transit toward another world:

> Marbles of the dancing floor
> Break bitter furies of complexity,
> Those images that yet
> Fresh images beget,
> That dolphin-torn, that gong-tormented sea.

"Byzantium" is a poem that deliberately blurs the line between natural and supernatural in accordance, as it were, with a line in the second of Yeats's "Supernatural Songs": "Natural and supernatural with the self-same ring are wed." It "hail[s] the superhuman," calling it indistinguishably "death-in-life" and "life-in-death." Yeats (unlike Coleridge) did not wish to separate them, for, as Helen Vendler comments, the intertwining of mental life and mental death-in-life was for him a psychological discovery.[66] Nevertheless, and Vendler would be the first to say so, his symbolism is not finally esoteric. When Yeats wants in "Byzantium" to define qualities of "the superhuman," he attaches negation to *worldly* images. So we have "a mouth that has no moisture and no breath"; "flames that no faggot feeds nor steel has lit"; "an agony of flame that cannot singe a sleeve." In other words, we are still in the world of experience, but at its limit, at the utmost pitch of creative ecstasy, inevitably a time that cannot be prolonged.

"A Dialogue of Self and Soul" stages a debate between an ascetic's and a sensualist's approach to conflict (whose spokesmen are My Soul and My Self), between spiritual transcendence and the bravado of total acceptance of experience. And it chooses the latter. Debate effectively ceases after the first section of the two-part poem. In the second section only Self speaks, now beyond argument and chanting a credo. The chant is inspiring but perhaps equivocal too because there is a measure of self-intoxication in its grand rhetoric, especially in the often-quoted final stanza:

I am content to follow to its source
Every event in action or in thought;
Measure the lot; forgive myself the lot!
When such as I cast out remorse
So great a sweetness flows into the breast
We must laugh and we must sing,
We are blest by everything,
Everything we look upon is blest.

We have noticed already, and will notice further in *Purgatory,* how stubbornly Yeats wrestled with the idea of self-forgiveness, but we can't help seeing that the three stanzas leading up to the last make us doubt that remorse has really been cast out. The first of these speaks very feelingly of youthful toil, ignominy, and clumsiness, and the third's initial claim that "I am content to live it all again" is undercut when it goes on to say (giving us a more bitter picture of his relationship with Gonne than we found earlier):

if it be life to pitch
Into the frog-spawn of a blind man's ditch,
A blind man battering blind men;
Or into that most fecund ditch of all,
The folly that man does
Or must suffer, if he woos
A proud woman not kindred of his soul.

This does not seem quite a satisfactory lead-in to that resolving last stanza, and I find more sincerity in the poignant end to the second stanza of the lead-in: "And what's the good of an escape, / If honour find him in the wintry blast?"

Let us turn to another major poem, "Among School Children," that attempts an ecstatic override of the question in "A Cold Heaven." The first seven of its eight stanzas constitute a beautifully sustained and dramatized lament for the defeat of human expectation, and the last is perhaps the poet's most memorable evocation of that ideal state Yeats called Unity of Being. But that last stanza seems to come out of nowhere. How does the poem manage to reach its conclusion, beginning with the lines "Labour is blossoming or dancing where / The body; is not bruised to pleasure soul"? Does it mean "Labour *should be*," and so on, since the poem has so convincingly described the heartbreaking mockery that life makes of youthful hope and beauty? Thomas Parkinson, who has studied Yeats's revisions, calls our attention to the fact that the "first version end[s] coolly with the observation that the world of permanent forms mocks every great man and his enterprise, but in its final version tear[s] the fabric of its vision to permit the emergence of the symbolic tree." Parkinson concludes: "we can . . . ask why the moment of enraptured vision should be so brief, whether it does genuinely transcend the limits so fully and affectionately treated in the bulk of the poem. The poem flirts with the danger of casting doubt on its own resolutions."[67] Perhaps "Among School Children" is successful because in this last stanza we feel the implication of "Labour should be" inside the words "Labour is." In any case, the one thing Yeats cannot do successfully in this prophetic mode is, with cold anger, assert a contempt for death, as in "Blood and the Moon," "Death," and much of "Under Ben Bulben."

Some lines of "The Tower" are rather arrogant as well, but the poem is lightened by humor and modulates into a beautiful diminuendo in its closing movement. In fact, although I am focusing on the more uncompromising strand of the attitude toward death in Yeats's poetry, I am not forgetting that Yeats was also a sensitive, delicate elegist as in the finale of "The Tower," and in such poems as "Adam's Curse," "The Wild Swans at Coole," and "In Memory of Major Robert Gregory." These are poems that do accept loss, disappointment, and mortality gracefully and graciously. One of the oddest aspects of Yeats's complex sensibility is that he doesn't seem to have liked that accepting part of himself as well as the other. One senses this in "The Circus Animals' Desertion," which expresses anger, not humane acquiescence, regarding the thought that, ladderless, he must now write from the heart alone.

As Yeats moved into his last years, the motif of violence problematizes his work more than it did before. Some fierceness or frenzy had long been part of the Yeatsian signature but was usually absorbed by the mythic material (as in "The Second Coming" and "Leda and the Swan," where it served to adumbrate a revelation) so that it did not call special attention to the man apart from the work. But the late poems do divert our attention in this way. This is not to suggest that Yeats was a fascist. I am convinced by R. F. Foster that Yeats's "idealized authoritarianism" is not accurately described as fascism. Its main point of contact with fascism is a positive interest in eugenics, but for Yeats this had to do with his snobbish pride in his Anglo-Irish ancestry and his *aesthetic* dismay at democracy's inevitable tolerance of mediocrity, *not* with race hatred or political domination. Yeats himself aptly (and wittily) described his splenetic manifesto *On the Boiler* as "tory"—"so tory that there is not a tory in the world that will agree with it."[68]

I want to focus on one problematic late work, the short play *Purgatory,* a work that is concerned with the attempt to purify an error of "breeding," because it specifically carries his conception of the purgatorial myth a step or two beyond "The Cold Heaven" and really as far as he was able to carry it.

An old man, with his son, contemplates the ruins of the ancestral house in which he was conceived. It came to ruin because his mother, who died giving birth to him, had debased herself by marrying her groom, a lout who squandered her inheritance and burned down the house in his drunkenness. Now the old man beholds therein a vision of his dead mother and explains to his coarse and ignorant son that souls in purgatory come back to familiar spots in order to:

> Re-live
> Their transgressions, and that not once
> But many times; they know at last
> The consequence of those transgressions
> Whether upon others or upon themselves;
> Upon others, others may bring help,
> For when the consequence is at an end
> The dream must end; if upon themselves,
> There is no help but in themselves
> And in the mercy of God.

The old man apparently thinks of himself as someone who is able to end that "consequence," but then, as (unseen by the boy) he further envisions on this anniversary night his mother reliving the very sexual act that will result in his birth, he is troubled by a problem:

> she must live
> Through everything in exact detail,
> Driven to it by remorse, and yet
> Can she renew the sexual act
> And find no pleasure in it, and if not,
> If pleasure and remorse must both be there,
> Which is the greater?

In spite of this scruple, and provoked by a physical struggle with his son and by a vision of his drunken father, he stabs the son to death as he had once stabbed his father—only to discover that he is still haunted by his mother's ghost and so has not "finished all that consequence." In conclusion he can only cry out in futile prayer:

> O God,
> Release my mother's soul from its dream!
> Mankind can do no more. Appease
> The misery of the living and the remorse of the dead.

With the help of Sandra F. Siegel's description and analysis of the manuscript materials, I think we can judge with some confidence the two most important shifts of authorial purpose that occurred during the writing of *Purgatory*.[69] In what Siegel calls the "scenario" of the play, it is the old man himself, and not the mother or father, who is the pollutant whose evil must be purged. I suspect that this scenario of 1938 was drafted under the influence of the Oedipus plays of Sophocles, modern versions of which Yeats had recently composed. He was reacting, it seems to me, against a classic tragic denouement in which the protagonist achieves peace in submission to a fate beyond the power of his own will. In support of this inference, one may compare the two-stanza choral poem following Oedipus's last departure from the stage in Robert Fitzgerald's translation of *Oedipus at Colonus* with Yeats's 1934 "Version for the Modern Stage." In Fitzgerald's faithful translation we read: "Because his sufferings were great, unmerited and untold, / Let some just god relieve him from distress!" This becomes in Yeats's free translation: "And rest among his mighty peers at last, / For the entanglements of God are past." Again, Fitzgerald gives us: "Let the descent be clear

/ As Oedipus goes down among the ghosts / On those dim fields of underground that all men living fear. / Eternal sleep, let Oedipus sleep well!" By contrast, in Yeats we read about "the travel-broken shade of Oedipus / Through triumph of completed destiny / Into eternal sleep, if such there be." One can see that Yeats is playing down the relative helplessness of man and of human deference to the power of fate and the gods. *His* Oedipus has been entangled with God and will take his place among mighty peers. *His* Chorus makes no mention of man's fear of death but, instead, hails the triumph of completed destiny. And, instead of the prayerlike "let Oedipus sleep well," we get the skeptical "eternal sleep, if such there be."[70]

In short, the poet remains resistant to an imaginative alliance with the heart's defeat and endeavors to retain not only his desire but also the ideal object of desire. This difficult ambition is worked out in fantastic fashion in the late plays just preceding *Purgatory*, especially *A Full Moon in March* and *The Herne's Egg*, in which a sexually compelling but proudly pure woman (the Queen, Attracta) is brought into contact with the severed head of a singer or symbolic poet. In *Purgatory*, despite its supernatural machinery, Yeats was perhaps attempting to find a more explanatory denouement for a similar vision.

In stage two of the composition process, Siegel finds, it is the mother's spirit that is to be purged while the old man, no longer said to be evil, is to become the agent of that purifying process. (One remembers that the Old Man who speaks at the beginning of *The Death of Cuchulain*, written shortly after *Purgatory*, is an evident stand-in for Yeats himself.) Siegel tells us that Yeats inserted the word "transgression" in this version of the play,[71] a word that suggests (as "evil" does not) the possibility of a revocable act, a recoverable innocence. Vendler observes to similar purpose that the word "consequence," conspicuous in *Purgatory*, introduces a new element in Yeats's conception of purgatory developed over the years. It raises the possibility that a bit of plot action under the old man's control, the killing of the son, can achieve this desired cleansing of the mother's spirit.[72] But the killing of the son, like the momentary appearance of the father, is dramatically contrived and unfelt. What seems to have concerned the poet most at this stage of composition was ending the protagonist's misery, a result somehow connected with re-idealizing the female object of desire.

My guess is that Yeats turned away from this idealizing vision between the second and final stage of composition because of the rage he felt in the last year or two of his life at the political and social debasement he saw all around him. *Purgatory* was first printed in *On the Boiler*, a tract that welcomes actual violence rather than poetic or apocalyptic violence as in "The Second Coming" and "Leda and the Swan." Thomas Whitaker finds some dignity in the play's rationale by saying that the old man "seeks by violence to annihilate history," which makes *Purgatory* sound not so very different from those poems, but the mythic context that in the apocalyptic poems establishes the violent displacement of cycle by revelation is lacking.[73] Moreover, the final version of *Purgatory* alters the idealizing intention of the preceding version, although the knowingly futile prayer that ends the play softens its grim theme a little by implying that the poet himself can go no further. It reads like an admission of his inability to do more in a bad time.[74]

The advance of *Purgatory* over "The Cold Heaven" lies only in a clearer sense of the indivisible connection between misery (seeming to come from without) and regret/remorse (coming from within). In the play, "misery" does not really come from without, but it looks that way because the mother's transgression allows the protagonist no way to distinguish between regret/remorse and pleasure.[75] In much the same way, the speaker's authentic confusion at the end of "The Cold Heaven" (will he be punished forever?) seems to arise from the fact that his regret/remorse on Maud Gonne's account looks to be inseparable from his continuing imaginative need for her idealized presence, so that loss and gain are indivisible. "The Cold Heaven" of course belongs to an earlier time when the question, though already rather desperate, still seemed resolvable. At the end of his life, the sense of defeat is more bitterly expressed. But this was not because he had failed to solve the mystery of the afterlife, for Yeats's myth of purgatory always concerned emotional conflicts in the life he was living. "Per Amica Silentia Lunae" introduces Yeats's visionary philosophy, but the beauty of that essay has much to do with its abiding attachment to this world: "When life puts away her conjuring tricks one by one, those that deceive us longest may well be the wine-cup and the sensual kiss." It is the pleasure-affirming spirit of *this* sentiment that soured at the end.

Yeats's last play, *The Death of Cuchulain,* and the accompanying (and aesthetically superior) poem, "Cuchulain Comforted," make a last effort to look beyond death but do little more than hold up for us a passive heroic image. There is no struggle, no overcoming. Cuchulain is indifferent to his degrading death, awaiting a possible but not yet conceivable reincarnation. He has no role in modern history, and Yeats seems unwilling to make him exemplary although his women desire this. This purgatory might be called a late Romantic gesture, acknowledging the void without the will to manipulate it further.

Lawrence's Underworld

D. H. Lawrence was one of the last-born poets in English literature centrally indebted to the High Romantic tradition. One bit of supporting evidence for that opinion is that, from his early poems right through to the end of his career, he used the word "death" in a psychological-spiritual as well as a physical-material sense. For him it meant a richer and darker kind of *being* than common experience affords. Correspondingly, *non-being* meant not nonexistence but a state of mechanical nullity. The early poem "Snap-Dragon," describing a darkly sexual encounter, ends with the affirming line, "And death, I know, is better than not to be."[76] "I can feel myself unfolding in the dark sunshine of death" is a characteristic line from a late poem.[77]

As Lawrence's vision matured, the movement into "death" came to be understood as a dynamic process promising the possibility of rebirth, a stripping away of some obstructive crust releasing an "under" or "blood" consciousness. But this more vital consciousness is always associated with darkness. In "New Heaven and Earth," for example, the reborn self is represented as dark and unknown, kindled at "the core of utter mystery."[78]

The close association of being with depth, darkness, and death is of course found in the novels as well as the poems. *Women in Love* is often explicit about a potentially rich psychological underworld: "[Ursula's] active living was suspended, but underneath, in the darkness, something was coming to pass." Similarly, Birkin instructs Gerald, "You've got to learn not-to-be, before you can come into being."[79] Learning not to be, like coming into being, is a deep life-experience, and easily distinguished from mere death, the physical extinction of a fictional character that a narrative sometimes requires.

Challenged by Enlightenment rationalism, the High Romantics felt the need to justify and enrich their conception of feeling and psychological depth. Wordsworth devised words and phrases like "undersoul," "purer being," "a motion and a spirit that impels all thinking things." Coming on the scene after the triumph of empirical science during the nineteenth century and specifically after psychoanalysis had begun to address emotional states in a scientific manner, Lawrence experienced the challenge even more keenly, and developed in response what Paul Eggert has called a "powerful vocabulary of the psychological underlife."[80]

This underlife must be carefully distinguished from Freud's unconscious. Lawrence did not seek to build on the Freudian unconscious, which he did not understand well, although some of his own insights have a psychoanalytic feel about them, like his famous distinction, in *Studies in Classic*

American Literature, between the overt intention of "the artist" and the covert drift of "the tale." He was seeking instead a non-Freudian or nonscientific way of thinking about *consciousness.* It was not his purpose to defend subjectivity because it was the very distinction between subjectivity and objectivity that was offensive. The critic Fiona Becket is right to say, "subjectivity is perhaps the notion that Lawrence is writing against."[81] One might add that his impulse to do so was more urgent precisely because his thinking approaches the psychoanalytic categories it resists.

In an almost absurdly ambitious effort to erase the gap grown wider during the nineteenth century between literal and metaphoric meaning, Lawrence in his mature work dispensed with splicing phrases like "as if" and "as though," which he had used in *Sons and Lovers,* and tried to think directly through metaphor.[82] Thus Rupert Birkin, looking at London outspread before him, remarks to Gerald Crich, "It's *real* death" (my emphasis).[83] Again, Ruskin's wife needn't have said, "John Ruskin should have married his mother," because "he *was* married to his mother" (Lawrence's emphasis).[84] Another good illustration comes from perhaps the finest of his late tales, a sharply revised version of Christ's resurrection. Lawrence's Christ, who repudiates his divine mission and discovers the natural world and the all-important mystery of touch, has returned from as literal a death as Lawrence can render without crossing the line into supernaturalism. He writes throughout of a man who *died,* although we are also reminded that this Christ was cut down too soon. Title and text insist as far as they can on a literal meaning of "died," and this is inseparable from the strength of the story, a story that conveys an experience of having been so *near* death that the return induces both nausea and a reawakened wonder, a coming back from so far away that the natural world seems to be perceived for the first time.

One may say, then, that the multiplication of Lawrencean terms to define the "underlife"—"pure inhuman otherness," "core of utter mystery," "mystic knowledge," "quick of death," "strong oblivion," "living dark," "dark sun," and many more—indicate, on the one hand, an awareness of the inescapability of metaphor but also, on the other, by their very insistence, an impatience with metaphor or at least a recognition of the sheer difficulty of trying to express the inexpressible. The same may be said of Lawrence's insistent use of certain adjectives to render the phenomenology of the psycho-spiritual underlife: glowing, glistening, flamy, shimmering, waving, cresting, flowing, wild, strange, soft, delicate, sensitive, suave, rich, full, electric, terrible, sharp, acute, violent, and a number of others. It's not an easy thing to convey a "palpable revelation of living otherness" as the novelist attempts to do in the "Excurse" chapter of *Women in Love*. Such experience is "never seen with the eye or known with the mind" yet seeks to be material and actual as well in that it is based on touch, for Lawrence the deepest of the senses.

Lawrence's rich underworld, like Rousseau's state of nature, is at once an indestructible core and, in the civilized world, a threatened and vulnerable bud. The contrast between civilized consciousness on the one hand and natural (or blood) consciousness on the other is similar in his thought and in Rousseau's. Lawrence in particular achieves some of his most striking effects in fiction and poetry by dramatizing the clash between the two kinds of consciousness. In "The Horse Dealer's Daughter," the young doctor who would like to keep his daily self intact is unsettled but also drawn out of his mechanical consciousness by the young woman's steady and dangerous eyes. He is literally drawn down by her into a muddy pond into which she had waded with a suicidal intention that he attempts to thwart. Her naïve but compelling claim on his love when he undresses her and brings her round is more than he can resist and he too falls in love, in spite of himself. So, in this unconventional tale of death and rebirth, both find themselves released from a superficial consciousness that is familiar and safe, then exposed to a deeper consciousness that is unfamiliar and frightening. The ending of the tale that clinches their "romance" is pointedly ironic:

> "I feel awful. I feel awful. I feel I'm horrible to you."
>
> "No, I want you, I want you," was all he answered, blindly, with that terrible intonation which frightened her almost more than her horror lest he should *not* want her.

Lawrence's myth of death and rebirth has here a complex, psychological character. It involves a clash between the dominant, customary self and the more vital but more hidden self. He wants his lovers to know fear of their unknown selves before they can experience tenderness and warmth.

There is something ambiguous, too, about the positive death associated with the Lawrencean underconsciousness. On the one hand, it is full, rich, pure in its otherness, wonderful in its dark mysteriousness, and so forth— the very antithesis of the mechanical nullity of the personal, all-too-human mental consciousness, the void of Hermione Roddice's chatter and Clifford Chatterley's published stories. (Ursula goes so far as to reflect: "In death we shall not be human, and we shall not know. The promise of this is our heritage, we look forward like heirs to their majority.")[85] On the other hand, by virtue of the very fact that there is so little meaningful outlet for a reborn consciousness in modern society, there may be something dangerous and unhealthy about such deep experience. In the premium it puts on depth, it runs the risk of isolating the individual. This aspect of the matter emerges in "Medlars and Sorb-Apples," in which imagery of vegetative decay and corruption is associated with a spiritual isolation that is both pure and unhealthy:

> Orphic farewell, and farewell, and farewell
> And the *ego sum* of Dionysos
> The *sono io* of perfect drunkenness
> Intoxication of final loneliness.[86]

The poem "Snake," like "The Horse Dealer's Daughter," dramatizes with effective irony and peculiar seductiveness the exposure of dangerous and deeper feeling to the familiar and timid everyday consciousness. In it, Lawrence opposes "the voice of my education," suspicious of underworlds, to a not so readily defined psychological underworld suggested by the snake's domain. In doing so, it seeks to contrast two kinds of knowing, civilized and primitive or neoprimitive. The Whitmanesque free verse, making use of well-paced and hypnotic repetition, attempts to re-create an older mode of thought, to show, as one critic put it, that "mythic modes of thought can be precisely a way of handling complex abstractions."[87]

The speaker describes an encounter in the Sicilian heat between a snake and himself at a water-trough. The beauty and dignity of the earth-golden, drinking snake and the respectful deference of the witness are established, but then "The voice of my education said to me / He must be killed, / For in Sicily the black, black snakes are innocent, the gold are venomous." The poem turns on the conflict between rational fear and the positive feeling aroused in the speaker by the snake's presence. Educated in fear, he throws a log toward the water-trough, whereupon the snake retreats into his hole "in undignified haste." But the other, less nameable voice stirs in him a feeling of shame for his petty act and even more of regret for it. For the snake seemed "Like a king in exile, uncrowned in the underworld, / Now due to be crowned again." In a phrase drawn perhaps from Emerson's essay "Experience," it is called one of the "lords of life" with whom the speaker has missed his chance.[88]

The word "underworld" is suggested in this poem by the snake's earthly hole, but for Lawrence a theory both of mind and history is entailed by it. Not unlike Yeats, Lawrence adopted a cyclical view of civilizations whereby a technologically advanced "white" civilization (Rome, America) had "repressed" an instinctively rich dark consciousness (Etruscan, Indian) that was bound to return in time and claim its inheritance. One of his late poems titled "Lucifer" starts out by quoting a line in *Macbeth*: "Angels are bright still, though the brightest fell." Then it grows querulous: "tell me, tell me, how do you know / he lost any of his brightness in the falling?"[89] Despite its obvious speculativeness, such vision does not lack a measure of psychological realism. The phallic consciousness symbolized by the snake *is* still in some sense repressed by a Christian civilization (more certainly *was* repressed in 1921 when the poem was written) and what is uneasily repressed may well return.

"Snake" belongs to a time in Lawrence's life when the social dimension of his view of death and rebirth was still important to him. But as his own death (in 1930) drew nearer—and during the last four or five years of his life he knew he was a dying man—this dimension recedes, and he wrote poems in which dying becomes a more intimate yet still life-affirming experience. This is implied to some extent in "The Man Who Died," but that tale is primarily allegorical. It is in the intimately personal late poems that Lawrence's imagining of death and dying is both most searching and most moving. I want to focus on two of these, "The Ship of Death" and "Bavarian Gentians."

From a purely rhetorical point of view, the best of the 108 lines in "The Ship of Death" are the first four:

Now it is autumn and the falling fruit
and the long journey towards oblivion.

The apples falling like great drops of dew
to bruise themselves an exit from themselves.

It is characteristic of Lawrence to derive even physical dying from individual will rather than from an external fate, and yet in these lines the process is impersonal and natural. The apples, re-creative in the very process of their disintegration, will eventually, like Shelley's autumnal West Wind, "quicken a new birth." No passage in the rest of the poem is at once so graceful and so concentrated, but Lawrence did work at revising the whole. And in doing so, as Helen Sword observes, he "excises virtually every negative image from the poem" and achieves "a serene sureness of purpose."[90] The result is that the several essential elements of his imagining of the end of life are distinctly illuminated.

The first of these is that dying is an extended process or experience oriented to the future. In borrowing the ship of death image from ancient Egyptian mythology, Lawrence shows no interest whatever in the idea of honoring a grave by placing an object in it that will carry deceased persons into an otherworld and will help to preserve them. His ship is purely symbolic and is *to be* built, in the mind. The stress falls on the slow effort of adjusting one's spirit to the fact of death, learning not just to accept but to *will* it. The unknown God that Lawrence evokes in these imaginings of death and dying is both present and absent, both expressible and inexpressible, like everything else in the Lawrencean depths. The speaker "knows" he will be in the hands of a God "unknown." The second major element is that death promises the boon of "oblivion," a word often associated with death in the Lawrencean oeuvre and used almost obsessively in these last poems. Its connotations are not negative. Oblivion for Lawrence does not imply obliteration but, rather, peace, cleansing, and renewal. And finally the poet emphasizes the emergence of a new morning and a new man. This idea of the resurrected body derives from Christianity, but the stress is not on spiritual triumph but on physical frailty, delicacy, and a new simplicity.

> The flood subsides, and the body, like a worn sea-shell
> emerges strange and lovely.
> And the little ship wings home, faltering and lapsing
> on the pink flood,
> and the frail soul steps out, into her house again
> filling the heart with peace.

The present tense is used, but this resurrected man is only to be glimpsed at the far end of an experience of forgetting. The poem then concludes by bringing us back to the process of dying itself, telling its readers (who are here joined with the speaker) that "the voyage of oblivion awaits you."

The finest of Lawrence's death poems is "Bavarian Gentians," and it deserves to be quoted in full:

> Not every man has gentians in his house
> In soft September, at slow, sad Michaelmas.
> Bavarian gentians, big and dark, only dark
> darkening the day-time, torch-like with the smoking blueness of
>   Pluto's gloom,
> ribbed and torch-like, with their blaze of darkness spread blue
> down-flattening into points, flattened under the sweep of white day
> torch-flower of the blue-smoking darkness, Pluto's dark-blue daze,

black lamps from the halls of Dis, burning dark blue,
giving off darkness, blue darkness, as Demeter's pale lamps give off
    light,
lead me then, lead the way.

Reach me a gentian, give me a torch!
let me guide myself with the blue, forked torch of this flower
down the darker and darker stairs, where blue is darkened on blue-
    ness
even where Persephone goes, just now, from the frosted September
to the sightless realm where darkness is awake upon the dark
and Persephone herself is but a voice
or a darkness invisible enfolded in the deeper dark
of the arms Plutonic, and pierced with the passion of dense gloom,
among the splendour of torches of darkness, shedding darkness on
    the lost bride and her groom.

The poem begins with a charming personal touch (gentians are rare in a sickroom) that yields gracefully, by way of alliteration and rhythmic retardation, to the image of the season that was Lawrence's favorite and one appropriate for its mythic occasion, Persephone's return to Pluto's underworld. Thereafter the speaker is scarcely personal. He becomes a venturer into a dark realm and witness of a mythic reunion. (Ronsard, more humane and less visionary, took a very different view of this reunion, writing that it was a slander to say that Pluto actually loved Proserpina, for such sweet feeling could not enter so hard a breast.) To enhance the effect of impersonality and wonder, Lawrence made three telling changes in revision. First, the poem no longer says, "whom have you come for," which is self-consciously personal, but "lead me then, lead the way," a more elevated phrase that helps to show the speaker's journey as symbolic and solemn. Second, instead of Persephone enfolded in "the arms of Pluto as he ravishes her once again," the revision describes her as "but a voice / or a darkness invisible enfolded in the deeper dark / of the arms Plutonic, and pierced with the passions of dense gloom." The implication of rape in the first version, which turns the speaker into an undignified voyeur, is deflected and made vague.[91] And third, the poem no longer ends with the speaker saying, self-consciously, that he will be a wedding-guest at the marriage of Pluto and Persephone but ends instead with the impressive and even poignant image of torches in the darkness "shedding darkness on the lost bride and her groom." In short, Lawrence uses the myth of Pluto and Persephone to render as literally as possible, for the reader as well as for the speaker, the experience of a symbolic underworld.[92]

In its hypnotic diction, the poem is doubtless a gamble with the limits of expressibility, but I think the gamble is successful in this case. Gentians are blue (the color of darkness in cinematography) and, being shaped somewhat like a flashlight, or what the English call a "torch," may be imagined as pointing ahead to give off faint or "dark" light. The slightly modified repetitions are not used to make distinctions but to intensify certain images, to fold them over on themselves, as it were. The most central image cluster is dark/darkness/darkening/darkened, intensified by repetition. A line like "darkness invisible enfolded in the deeper dark" might be compared to the union of Birkin and Ursula in *Women in Love*: "the body of mysterious night upon the body of mysterious night." In both the poem and the novel, Lawrence attempts to describe the indescribable, to express the inexpressible.

One probably cannot persuade those who believe such literary ambition doomed from the outset to change their minds. But in the context of this study I would defend Lawrence's experimental ineffability in this way. For earlier writers in the Romantic tradition, Nothingness or Void was terrifying, fascinating, or fruitful. Somehow or other it had to be challenged. Lawrence devised a further modification, which is to make "nothing" and "not nothing" mean much the same thing. (See the penultimate paragraph of *Sons and Lovers* for an early trial of this tactic.) He invests with numinous reality a number of negative or negative-sounding words—invisible, dark, unknown, sightless, other, inhuman. In a poem like "Bavarian Gentians," he thus creates a neo-Romantic myth of an underworld, fusing the immaterial and the palpable, nothing and something.

The Meaningless Void

Mid-Twentieth Century to the Present

I do not propose in this study to engage the ongoing debate concerning modernism versus postmodernism. But the particular subject matter I am addressing does bring forward a different and to some extent competing literary periodization of the last century. My previous chapter slid across the break in sensibility often said to have occurred around 1910. As different in some respects as Yeats and Lawrence were from Tennyson, Dickinson, and Housman, my particular viewpoint highlighted the resemblances among them. All of these poets were skeptical about the Christian afterlife, but all resisted a purely agnostic view and sought some kind of alternative mythology to satisfy their highly individualistic sensibilities. This chapter, similarly, does not imply a dating of modernism along traditional lines but suggests that an important shift of sensibility *did* occur at about the midpoint of the twentieth century. Focusing on poetic imaginings of the end of life, I mark this shift between the age of Yeats and Lawrence on the one hand and the age of late Stevens, Bishop, and Larkin on the other. The poets to be studied in this chapter, whether favorably inclined toward religion or not, share a sensibility that is scarcely apparent earlier. Although any single date is too specific, the change becomes discernible about the end of World War II and dominant by the sixties.

I can dramatize this change of *mentalité* by calling attention to an anomalous feature of it. There come readily to mind several literary landmarks published between 1931 and 1951 that seemed at the time to feature a "modern" approach to the subject of death, but this feature of them now resembles the confrontational approach characteristic of the Romantic period. In terms of my argument, they exemplify a neo-Romantic resistance to the void much more than a late modernist recognition of the meaningless void. The first is Virginia Woolf's *The Waves* (1931), whose central character, Bernard, declares on the book's last page: "Against you I will fling myself, unvanquished and unyielding, O Death!" The second is the work (considered as a whole) of Albert Camus and Jean-Paul Sartre that was published around World War II that established a worldwide vogue for existentialism. This popular philosophy highlighted the heroic opposition of the solitary soul to the inexorable fact of death. It taught that awareness of and resistance to this reality determined the morality of our choices and the authenticity of our lives. Last, I am thinking of Dylan Thomas's celebrated villanelle of 1951, "Do Not Go Gentle into That Good Night," whose title (repeated of course in refrains, along with the line "Rage, rage against the dying of the light") sounds rather like the old Promethean stance discussed in chapter 3. Wanting us to admire this poem, Seamus Heaney asks us to consider it in another light, as "the protest of the poet's child-self against . . . the father's remoteness."[1] This is a fresh and welcome interpretation, but Heaney offers it precisely as a way of defending the poem against the charge of posturing. Other advanced readers (like James Merrill, in his poem "Losing the Marbles") have gently mocked its posturing tone and, a little sadly, since it was once a favorite, I'm inclined to agree with them.

This is not to say that the word "existential," if we can separate it from the Sartrean philosophy with which it is associated, has quite lost relevance. An existential view of death, minus the heroics, has so permeated contemporary consciousness that most serious writers and readers today are unofficial existentialists. That is, the word no longer distinguishes much. As this chapter will imply, it doesn't even distinguish clearly a religious from a secular worldview.

Despite many kinds of stylistic differences among the seven poets considered in this chapter, their imaginings of the end of life share certain specific and telling characteristics. One is a new absence of curiosity about what follows death, a subject that no longer is regarded as a part of life. Another is a shift of attention from death itself to the prospect of death, which unquestionably *is* a part of life and an important part. The shift entails a more self-conscious use of metaphor on the part of poets who now associate such images as darkness, stillness, coldness, and emptiness not with death but with the fading of consciousness. And finally, there is in these poems a quieter, less heroic tone of address, a resistance to the kind of overtly expressed consolation clinched by a meaningful, weighted conclusion. Instead, we find a cooler consolation implicit in the conduct of the voice as it shies away from conclusiveness. Yeats at the end of his life foresaw truly, though with dismay, that "the romantic cult of personality" was dying and that the poetry to come would feature "finely articulated fact."[2]

The transition to this new sensibility might almost be signaled by one poem, Stevens's "The Idea of Order at Key West" (1935), a work that considers the point at which the human voice vanishes into inhuman sound. This poem is sometimes said to be a twentieth-century version of Wordsworth's "The Solitary Reaper." Such a coupling warrants the suggestion that the later poem not only reaches into the silence like the earlier one but also shows how the poetry of the future will demand of the poet a new precision in recognition of a new sense of difficulty. Stevens's poem—particularly its concluding line, "In ghostlier demarcations, keener sounds"—prepares us to expect from new imaginings of the end of life a subtler consolation crafted from the prospect of an event that has lost the moral significance it once had.

Wallace Stevens: "The ever-never-changing same"

I start with Stevens (1879–1955), the only one of the poets to be discussed in this chapter who was born in the nineteenth century but whose late poems—including in particular several fine "death poems"—provide an ideal point of entry. Stevens's stance had all along been naturalistic, quietly but firmly putting aside whatever official religion had to say about death and the afterlife. But his humanism was of the expansive type—like Emerson's and Whitman's—which means that even the most explicitly naturalistic affirmations in *Harmonium* (like the marvelous final stanza of "Sunday Morning") had the sort of rhetorical grandeur that is perhaps closer to the post-Romantic rhetoric featured in the preceding chapter than to his own late style. The late poems are less flamboyant, brilliant in a subtler way, and they have not lacked for appreciation. I want to consider here just three of them, which, both in what they say and don't say, exemplify a new way of looking at the end of life.

First, "The Course of a Particular":

Today the leaves cry, hanging on branches swept by wind,
Yet the nothingness of winter becomes a little less.
It is still full of icy shades and shapen snow.

The leaves cry . . . One holds off and merely hears the cry.
It is a busy cry, concerning someone else.
And though one says that one is part of everything,

There is a conflict, there is a resistance involved;

And being part is an exertion that declines:
One feels the life of that which gives life as it is.

The leaves cry. It is not a cry of divine attention,
Nor the smoke-drift of puffed-out heroes, nor human cry.
It is the cry of leaves that do not transcend themselves,

In the absence of fantasia, without meaning more
Than they are in the final finding of the ear, in the thing
Itself, until, at last, the cry concerns no one at all.[3]

A poem by Stevens is often difficult to get an interpretive handle on, partly because the title may offer no immediate clue as to what it's about. (In this case the meaning of the enigmatic title becomes apparent later.) But the primary reason is that the emotion or emotional situation involved must be inferred from the kind of thing being described (for example, leaves crying) and from the subtle modulations of this description. To say that leaves cry (rather than, perhaps, rustle) is to attribute to the leaves, if not a certain emotion, at least the power to make a human appeal. The appeal here is ineffectual, whether we understand the second line to mean that the nothingness of winter becomes *only* or *even* a little less. The human mind either cannot respond to the cry (it concerns "someone else") or will not ("there is a resistance involved").

As in many poems by Stevens, there is interplay between mind and world, imagination and reality, and the mind's participatory role is of course crucial. "One feels the life of that which gives life as it is" becomes his equivalent to Wordsworth's "half create and half perceive." But in the last six lines this subjective element appears to be removed, for the poem in its severe restraint follows as objectively as possible the course of a particular "particular," the crying leaves. The leaves merely cry, a cry that reaches nothing and no one beyond the leaves. Finally, however, it becomes clear that the pseudo-objective statement "the cry concerns no one at all" is to be explained by an absence of imaginative participation, by a subjective or emotional blank in "the final finding of the ear." The seemingly unimportant phrase in the last line—"until, at last"—indicates that a process or "course" has been involved in the determination of this meaningless cry, and it is necessarily a human process. The mind in its decline offers the world less and less until, at last, it comes to believe what has always been the plain truth, that the world means nothing in itself without the involvement of human interest. Unlike most of the poems discussed in the previous chapter, this one does not appear to be about the approach of death, but it is, profoundly so. One has only to shift one's attention from the body to consciousness.

Here is another of Stevens's death poems, "Of Mere Being," placed at the end of his last published volume.

The palm at the end of the mind,
Beyond the last thought, rises
In the bronze decor,

A gold-feathered bird
Sings in the palm, without human meaning,
Without human feeling, a foreign song.

You know then that it is not the reason
That makes us happy or unhappy.
The bird sings. Its feathers shine.

The palm stands on the edge of space.
The wind moves slowly in the branches.
The bird's fire-fangled feathers dangle down.

In this case the title is readily suggestive. The poet is seeking the mereness of being, an approach to meaninglessness this side of death. But the technique employed is inventively different from that in "The Course of a Particular." This poem is only marginally about the interplay of mind and world. The palm and the gold-feathered bird singing in the palm are inside the mind, "at the end of the mind, / Beyond the last thought, ris[ing] / In the bronze decor." At the center of the poem there is interplay of another kind, furnished by the fact that its imagery is meant to remind the reader of Stevens's more exuberant earlier poems. The speaker can of course recall these images but cannot summon any longer the emotion that was once attached to them, and so is obliged to realize that it is not images in themselves that make us happy or unhappy. The poem's severe simplicity of style, its husks of elements that once generated lively desire, carry the emotional burden, a quiet descent to darkness on *unextended* wings. Gold coloring, palm, bird, and fire are familiar images evoking desire in its more youthful manifestations, but the poem is seeking the end of desire, mere being. The bird sings, the palm stands, the wind moves. And the last line captures one last gaudy flourish, "fire-fangled feathers," before checking it by another alliteration suggestive of sexual finality, "dangles down." The poem contains no hint of transcendence, protest, or even acquiescence. Yet it moves us by extending our sense of the human into the space of the inhuman, by its way of leaning against a void.

One more poem by Stevens, this one unpublished in his lifetime but evidently belonging to his last period (1947–55). Despite its understatement and its subtly developed affirmation, it is also a death poem, as is implied by its charming title, "As You Leave the Room":

You speak. You say: Today's character is not
A skeleton out of its cabinet. Nor am I.

That poem about the pineapple, the one
About the mind as never satisfied,

The one about the credible hero, the one
About summer, are not what skeletons think about.

I wonder, have I lived a skeleton's life,
As a disbeliever in reality,

A countryman of all the bones in the world?
Now, here, the snow I had forgotten becomes

Part of a major reality, part of
An appreciation of a reality

And thus an elevation, as if I left
With something I could touch, touch every way.

And yet nothing has been changed except what is
Unreal, as if nothing had been changed at all.

The gentle title allows for a touch of drama, the poet regarding himself about to depart a living space and then, via the italicized opening, turning over the speaking of the poem to his departing self. This speaker insists with a touch of feistiness that he is not a skeleton because the subjects of his previous poems (we are meant, of course, to catch the allusions to these) "are not what skeletons think about." Still, he can wonder whether he has lived a skeleton's life, recognizing a long-standing distinction between thinking about things (which has enchanted him) and things in themselves (so-called reality, in which he has disbelieved). But—without using any word such as "but" and even in the middle of a couplet—he turns upon this scruple and affirms that a heightened "appreciation of reality" should not be distinguished from reality itself, from "something I could touch, touch every way." This is not, however, a simple collapse of the categories that had sustained Stevens's work throughout his career, Imagination (the "Unreal") and Reality. The twice-repeated phrase "as if" suggests clearly enough that, since neither "unreal" nor "real" has meaning except in relation to the other, you could say "nothing has been changed at all." Or you could say (because the mind is always changing and running the gamut of emotion between fullness and emptiness) that the categories have been temporarily collapsed, and either Imagination or Reality has in the meantime taken over. The little word "As" in the title looks, in retrospect, very important. "As one leaves" means one has not finally left, and so the mind through the gamut of its moods will be in process and at play. A Dickinson poem often seeks out the sudden, timeless recognition of the moment of death, but the last word for Stevens as death approaches can only be an affirmation of the mind's process itself, with all the complexity that "process" implies.

Those last two lines of "As You Leave the Room" not only tell us a lot about Stevens but also tell us something about the style of imagining the end of life that began to assume predominance around the middle of the twentieth century. Change is the law of life, we say, but change in this poem is not being contrasted to changelessness, as life may be contrasted to death. No myth of a timeless afterlife is in the picture. For Stevens, change means verbal and imaginative process, and *that*, as far as the mind can know, is always happening, always the case. ("It Must Change" is one of the headings of "Notes toward a Supreme Fiction.") Yet these are mental, intangible changes. Poetic process must feed on the tangible world, on reality, on that which is *there* or *given* and so in a sense does not change. For Stevens, then, changelessness is indissolubly joined with change in human experience. The diminution that comes with aging is real enough, but it involves no dramatic disjuncture (like the cessation of consciousness), only more subtle descriptions of consciousness, more precise and scrupulous language.

In one of his later volumes, *Transport to Summer*, Stevens wrote an "Adult Epigram" defining "the romance of the precise" that he sought to capture in verse. He called it "the ever-never-changing same, / An appearance of Again, the diva-dame." This epitomizes one of his most important poetic discoveries. The mind, he came to understand, is always changing, and *that* is its very principle of constancy. To be always changing is to be always the same. And this insight bears directly on the fact that the modern poetic consciousness turns away from the subject of death and focuses instead on the end of life. Stevens might have been reading Wittgenstein's "Tractatus"

(6.431)—"in death . . . the world does not change, but ceases"—although he doubtless came to this discovery on his own. The poet, like the philosopher, realized that the void of death offers nothing to the imagination, and strictly speaking is meaningless. In prospect of the end of life, one finds a subtler, less combative voice against the void, responding to the recognition of ghostlier demarcations with keener sounds.

Elizabeth Bishop: Seeing and Not Seeing

Elizabeth Bishop was born in 1911 and published her important first volume *North and South* (which contains all of the poems I will comment on) in 1946. Her appreciative but wary way of looking at the world, resulting in subtle modes of irony, suited well the postwar mood of American poetry. Her skill in describing detail owes much to that of Marianne Moore, but Moore's descriptions are linked always to a defense against outer danger, whereas Bishop's, influenced perhaps by Dickinson as well as by her own traumatic early experience, are linked to inner danger.[4] Bishop took the visible world too seriously to be as openly ironic about her own experience as, say, Philip Larkin or Howard Nemerov often were. Although she described herself as "not religious," explaining that "modern religiosity in general . . . always seems to lead to a tone of moral superiority,"[5] she liked the creation-praising religious verse of Herbert and Hopkins. But her own poems almost always create a sense of distance between the poet and what she is describing, as if she felt she didn't quite belong in the world, as if she found the world strange and disturbing as well as fascinating in its very actuality.

Her imaginative eye, then, is both risk-taking and fearful, making more acute both the desire to see and not to see.[6] Bishop, like Stevens, is curious about consciousness rather than about an afterlife but focuses her sense of complexity on "seeing" as he does on "change." For Stevens the hedonistic stoic, the thought of death leads to meditation on the relation between change and changelessness. For Bishop the sensitive ironist, it both sharpens the eye and disturbs the mind, augmenting the tension between seeing and not seeing.

If she did not write a death-of-self poem strictly speaking, she wrote at least several ("The Unbeliever," "The Man-Moth," "Cootchie") that concern death, and do so in an intimate way. They tell us something as well about contemporary deployment of point of view and imagery in poems that imagine the end of life.

"The Unbeliever" begins with an epigraph from John Bunyan—"He sleeps on the top of a mast"—and proceeds:

He sleeps on the top of a mast
with his eyes fast closed.
The sails fall away below him
like the sheets of his bed,
leaving out in the air of the night the sleeper's head.

Asleep he was transported there,
asleep he curled
in a gilded ball on the mast's top,
or climbed inside
a gilded bird, or blindly seated himself astride.

"I am founded on marble pillars,"
said a cloud. "I never move.
See the pillars there in the sea?"
Secure in introspection
he peers at the watery pillars of his reflection.

A gull had wings under his
and remarked that the air
was "like marble." He said: "Up here
I tower through the sky
For the marble wings on my tower-top fly."

But he sleeps on the top of his mast
with his eyes closed tight.
The gull inquired into his dream,
which was, "I must not fall.
The spangled sea below wants me to fall.
It is hard as diamonds; it wants to destroy us all."[7]

Bunyan's Christian tells Simple, Sloth, and Presumption, "You are like them that sleep on the top of a mast, for the Dead Sea is under you." Bunyan means that their vices will lead them to certain hell. The predicament of Bishop's "unbeliever" is considerably more complex. Yes, the world he sees in his dream is hostile, even deadly, and not just for himself ("it wants to destroy us all"), but his dream also expresses a wish, a wish to court risk, to look at danger. Unbelief in this context implies the excitement of doing so, and, as Robert Dale Parker comments, "primes [the poet's] vision."[8] Unbelief means keeping options open, whereas a believer like Bunyan holds to some definite truth. Probably Bishop was alluding also to Melville's imaginative Ishmael, who enjoys his reverie atop the mast while cautioning himself that one dreamy step can prove fatal.

The unbeliever is contrasted in the course of the poem to a cloud and a gull. To be sure, his eyes are "fast shut" (a fact twice noted), but in another and more restrictive sense so are theirs. The cloud and the gull are too confident in their own beliefs. The cloud evades fear of destruction and death by being "secure in introspection," so blindly self-confident that he mistakes his reflection in the sea for "marble pillars" on whose solid strength he is "founded." The gull evades fear by being so blindly self-confident in the power of his aspiration that he thinks his reflected wings and the air through which they fly have the indomitable strength of marble. Their failure to see truly is evident: the cloud thinks he is not moving because his reflection does not appear to move; the gull thinks he has the strength to fly forever. The unbeliever, of course, also practices a strategy of evasion—sleep—on the face of it a more cowardly form of evasion because it is plainly chosen. But his dream reports a truth that the others do not face.

Bishop, then, is using the old idea of a true dream to express a complex reality. The result of living in the world is predictable enough (we will all fall eventually), but we experience our living as strange. (Two poems that shortly follow this one in *North and South*, "Sleeping on the Ceiling" and "Sleeping Standing Up," playing with a similar image, combine strangeness with ordinariness.) The unbeliever looks *away from* but also *at* what he fears. And this, she implies, is what the poet also does. This is not to say that unbelief becomes simply another kind of belief. The poet feels a certain tenderness for the unbeliever not bestowed on the others, but she is less interested in saying who's right than in showing that all observation is a matter both of seeing and not seeing at the same time. Bishop's poems, David Kalstone commented, "both describe and set themselves at the limit of description."[9]

That she finds aspects of the visible world more or less attractive but does not press for moral judgments of them is brought out by another poem, similarly parabolic, called "Seascape." The seascape first appears to the single speaker as "celestial . . . with white herons got up as angels," like a "cartoon by Raphael for a tapestry for a Pope." But in the second half of the poem the speaker notices "a skeletal lighthouse standing there / in black and white clerical dress" and "thinks that hell rages below his iron feet." Clearly,

Bishop finds (and expects us to find) the first seascape more attractive, morally as well as aesthetically, but she lets this remain implied at the level of seeing, without drawing a moral.

The implied tenderness for the unbeliever and preference for the first seascape are important nonetheless because they tell us what as readers we are being asked ultimately to feel about poetry. This comes out most clearly in the surrealistic poem "The Man-Moth," the account of a humanoid creature who, like the unbeliever, is beset by imaginative anxiety but with whom Bishop identifies even more closely. It is a poem that looks deeply inward and also one that illuminates her work generally, showing in particular that for this poet the mental eye is as important as the physical eye famously on display in "The Fish" and "Rooster."

The Man-Moth might be called dreaming man, a creature whose fantastic actions are seemingly but not actually self-destructive. He is a sort of night-wanderer, looking down from above at "battered moonlight," then up from the sidewalk at a fearfully "small hole at the top of the sky." He "nervously begins to scale the faces of the buildings." "He trembles, but must investigate as high as he can climb." What we understand most clearly is that he is profoundly frightened and yet compelled *by* his fear to act: "what the Man-Moth fears most he must do." The unusual wording that puts "most" and "must" (similar sounds belonging to antithetical phrases) into the closest possible contiguity stresses the ambivalence that Bishop is dramatizing.

Two more stanzas highlight both the magnitude of the Man-Moth's fear and his compulsion to subject himself to this fear. He always "travels backwards" on the subway, "does not dare look out the window," and "has to keep / his hands in his pockets." Further, "he must / be carried through artificial tunnels and dream recurrent dreams." But in the final stanza Bishop reveals her particular tenderness for this creature and clarifies his symbolic importance. The stanza tells us that if we look closely at his dark-as-night eye, we will discover "one tear, his only possession"; if we're not paying attention, "he'll swallow it," but, if we are watching, "he'll hand it over / cool as from underground springs and pure enough to drink." That is to say, he is like a poet whose courageous exploration of the mind's depth is in a sense private, yet, if *we* are sensitive to her, she can grant us healing and support.

One more poem by Bishop that I want to examine is "Cootchie," a work seldom discussed, perhaps because it seems on the surface merely comic and a bit patronizing, but in fact it repays analysis. (One ready index of its complexity is that "Cootchie" is much more intricate in rhyme, rhythm, diction, and tone than are the related "Songs for a Colored Singer" that follow it in *North and South* and come out of the same years, the Florida years, of Bishop's experience.) Although this poem is technically an elegy, the fictional Cootchie is hardly mourned as the subject of an elegy would be. She serves rather as an emblem of human unimportance and is handled by the poet in a way that reveals something about the way later twentieth-century poets imagine the end of life.

> Cootchie, Miss Lula's servant, lies in marl,
> black into white she went
>   below the surface of the coral-reef.
> Her life was spent
>   in caring for Miss Lula, who is deaf,
> eating her dinner off the kitchen sink
> while Lula ate hers off the kitchen table.
> The skies were egg-white for the funeral
>   and the faces sable.
>
> Tonight the moonlight will alleviate
> the melting of the pink wax roses
>   planted in tin cans filled with sand
> placed in a line to mark Miss Lula's losses;
>   but who will shout and make her understand?
> Searching the land and sea for someone else,
> The lighthouse will discover Cootchie's grave
> and dismiss all as trivial; the sea, desperate,
>   will proffer wave after wave.

The first stanza is a comic account of Cootchie's life and death, distancing with wit the pity we are prepared to feel for someone whose life was one of utter social subordination and devoted service to the hard-of-hearing Miss Lula. But the comedy lacks satirical edge, allowing the second stanza (perfectly parallel to the first in its intricate and quite unconventional rhyme scheme yet very different in tone) to recover a modicum of pathos for Cootchie and to expand effortlessly into a much broader view of her death. The ludicrous name of the servant was probably assigned to her by her mistress (though, in the patronizing society reflected by it, no disparagement need have been intended). She lies unceremoniously in marl, a whitish mixture of clays and shells, but while this suggests indignity, the poet's interest appears to focus on the black-white contrast itself, a contrast whose tone and effect are repeated at the end of the stanza as the funeral is described in terms of "egg-white" skies versus the "sable" faces of the (probably official) few who attended it.

Bishop observed of poetry in general that "switching tenses always gives effects of depth, space, foreground, background, and so on . . . like switching keys in music,"[10] and indeed the switch from present to future tense in the brilliant second stanza of this poem accomplishes these effects. Instead of the first stanza's lightly ironic but direct description of a human scene, we rise in the second beyond that human scene and are invited to adopt the perspective of three large, inhuman agencies—the moonlight, the light-house, and the sea—imagined as taking some sort of interest in the after-math of Cootchie's death. The moonlight, cooler than sunlight, will retard the melting of the wax roses that presumably signify Miss Lula's modest mourning gesture, but it can do no more; it cannot certainly bring back a shouting Cootchie to help her deaf mistress to understand. The light from the lighthouse will circle round land and sea as if searching for someone else, someone more important; it will inevitably in this search pass across Cootchie's grave but find nothing significant. And the sea, humanized to the point of being said to be "desperate," will make what resembles an earnest gesture of grief, proffering "wave after wave." But (the pathos reduced by a pun) it is merely breaking "wave after wave" on the shore, as it has always impersonally done.

The moonlight, the lighthouse, and the sea are Cootchie's real mourners, but they cannot reach her and of course do not mourn in any meaningful human sense. Bishop employs pathetic fallacy not to suggest that the natu-ral or material world is sympathetically connected to the human world but to heighten the impersonality of this particular event. Yet it is not altogether impersonal. The moonlight, the lighthouse, and the sea seem to be looking intently, even describing intently what they see, as if trying to find some-thing and failing. These agencies illustrate both Bishop's remarkable skill in seeing what's before us and her equally remarkable candor in *trying* to see what is hidden and disturbing, at bottom our fear of death. Since death is involved, she is drawn inevitably to such traditional images as distant light and the sea, but she cannot say, like Arthur Hugh Clough, "Westward, look, the land is bright" or, like Tennyson, "When that which drew from out the boundless deep / Turns again home." As a contemporary poet she must be more self-conscious about the use of light and sea metaphors, more aware of their inadequacy in expressing consolation.

Bishop once said, "One can never have too many defenses."[11] This seems the statement of a timid person, but the very candor of it and its touch of irony (for we catch in its phrasing the intent of overstatement) show us that this poet is aware of her vulnerability and also courageous enough to probe some of those defenses. The fear of death spurs Bishop's unbeliever, Man-Moth, and moonlight-lighthouse-sea to look hard, but it also leads to evasion, illusion, and failure, and these are recorded for us as part of the whole truth. Free of cynicism though not of irony, Bishop's art demonstrates that seeing and not seeing are equally part of the human situation.

The Originality of Philip Larkin's "Nothing"

His biographer Andrew Motion nicely epitomizes the history of Larkin's reputation: "*The Less Deceived* [1955] made his name; *The Whitsun Weddings* [1964] made him famous; *High Windows* [1974] turned him into a national monument."[12] The first title points to one of the important reasons for Larkin's wide appeal, which is shared by a sufficient number of advanced readers not to be bogus. The poet is "less deceived" in that he is suspicious of sanguine hopes, rhetorical inflation, mystification of any kind. Like his principal model, Thomas Hardy, he is ready to forgo consolation and accept unhappiness. (In an interview, Larkin ventured to say, "writing about unhappiness is probably the source of my popularity.")[13] The impression of honesty we get from these poems is enhanced by the fact that the speaker often questions himself, debates with himself on behalf of his readers. He likes to use the pronoun "we," seeking our agreement, as he makes the kind of moral generalization he favors. He is too earnest to be fairly called a satirist, although he is witty and certainly capable of satirical swipes. "To be a satirist," he said, "you have to think you know better than everyone else. I've never done that."[14]

Nor is he quite a pessimist, a word that would fail to describe the peculiar tension and emotional weight of the better poems, despite their resistance to consolation. The widely known "Church Going" is swathed in ironies, to be sure, but the poem arises from "a hunger in himself to be more serious." The "dying fall" we find in "Dockery and Son," which ends with the line "And age, and then the only end of age" is earned, for the poem is active with the energy of internal debate. Larkin's poems are full of connectives such as "yes, but," "no, then," "so," "in short," "even so," "in fact," and "perhaps," indicating that he is wrestling with himself on some intimate subject, often sociability versus solitariness or the pros and cons (mostly cons) of marriage, a conflict Larkin never resolved but the dramatic potential of which he learned to exploit. "The Whitsun Weddings" patiently and characteristically accumulates detail about ordinary life and common hopes and then renders judgment in the form of an ambiguous image: "And as the tightened brakes took hold, there swelled / A sense of falling, like an arrow-shower / Sent out of sight, somewhere becoming rain." Is this a picture of marriage as blessing or curse or something elusive that could point in either direction? "Talking in Bed" also leads *its* ordinary situation toward a finely ambiguous conclusion: "It becomes still more difficult to find / Words at once true and kind, / Or not untrue and not unkind."[15]

Because critics have associated Larkin with the literary school known as "The Movement,"[16] and also because of his own misleading disparagement of Yeatsian rhetoric (misleading in that traces of his initial attraction to that grandeur remain in *his* music), Larkin's style of plain speaking has not always been appreciated. It is not exactly *plain*. Yes, his language is sometimes conversational in tone, often enough laced with colloquialism and racy slang, but it is also graceful, intricate in its patterns (patterns that do not force themselves on our attention), concentrated, and, above all, memorable. Although the poems often deal with common predicaments, the anguish of these predicaments is inexplicable except on the assumption that the poet himself is not content with commonplace language or attitudes. Some poems (like the famous or notorious "This Be the Verse") contain coarse diction, but, as Motion observed, "it was entirely characteristic for Larkin to combine delicacy and coarseness."[17] Thus, while the first stanza of "This Be the Verse" begins with the shock-line, "They fuck you up, your mum and dad," the first line of the second stanza, "But they were fucked up in their turn," is cleverly scrupulous and sensitive. Larkin could also shift the diction of a whole poem from demotic to lyrical, as in "High Windows," to be discussed later.

Since he writes with particular energy about the fear of death and does not hesitate to suggest that the cessation of consciousness voids meaning, I am especially concerned that we do not underrate the complexity and the emotional pressure of these poems. The short "Nothing To Be Said" asserts simply, "Life is slow dying" and concludes with apparent simplicity: "And saying so to some / Means nothing; others it leaves / Nothing to be said." The power of that last "Nothing" would be lost without the contrast to the preceding, flat "nothing" that reflects the common attitude. Larkin's Nothing (like Beckett's) is a "something," a force that infects our living and that (as another poem, "I Remember, I Remember," puts it) "happens anywhere."

Larkin wants to shock us but not into a state of spiritual awe as Dickinson does. Rather, he seeks to impress an awareness of emptiness upon us. The poem "Next, Please" eerily calls this emptiness "a huge and birdless silence." (Possibly this alludes to the Greek-derived word for the underworld, "avernus," meaning "birdless"; according to legend, the Lake of Avernus, because it lay just above the underworld, sent up such toxic fumes that no birds could fly near it.)

Using words to evoke silence is a paradoxical ambition, and doing it well calls for unusual resourcefulness. Seamus Heaney wrote (disparagingly) of "High Windows": "When Larkin lifts his eyes from nature, what appears is a great absence."[18] I take this to be an unintended tribute to his originality. Like other later twentieth-century poets, Larkin imagines the end of life by emptying the resonance latent in certain images, but he also tries to magnify the image of emptiness itself. The silence in "Next, Please" is not only "birdless" but also "huge." In the poem called "Absences," the speaker lifts his vision "above the sea," above "the yet more shoreless day," as if emptying out the whole phenomenal world—and then cries out in an ecstatic final line, set off from the preceding ones, "Such attics cleared of me! Such absences!" The last line of "High Windows" is similarly eloquent in its very negativity: it speaks of a "nothing" and a "nowhere" that is *endless* (my emphasis).

For whatever psychological reasons, Larkin's poems are shadowed by the idea of death. We are reminded again and again of death's nearness, inevitability, and utter finality. In poems like "Next, Please," "The Old Fools" and "Aubade," Larkin proves himself to be a master of the mordant mood, combining anger at our self-deception with admission of his own fear of death. In others, like "Wants, "Here," and "High Windows," the thought of oblivion seems relatively attractive, free of anxiety at any rate. To compass the range of this poet's imagining of death, I want to focus on one poem from each group ("Aubade" and "High Windows"), with passing references to the others.

"Next, Please," for all its macabre seductiveness, comes close to being a cynical poem, undermining all human hopes and endeavors.[19] But when Larkin began to engage with the matter of death at closer quarters, visiting the home where his aged mother, stricken with Alzheimer's disease, had been placed, his anger and fear became more urgent and more complex. To one correspondent, Larkin commented on this complexity in "The Old Fools": "It's rather an angry poem but the anger is ambivalent—we are angry at the humiliation of age, but we are also angry at old people for reminding us of death."[20] The latter kind of anger, so biting that it seems cruel, is what we first notice as we read this poem. But the speaker's own fears become apparent as we move from the first to the second stanza, and these fears contribute to the poem's intensity.

> What do they think has happened, the old fools,
> To make them like this? Do they somehow suppose
> It's more grown-up when your mouth hangs open and drools,
> And you keep on pissing yourself, and can't remember
> Who called this morning?
> . . . . .
> Why aren't they screaming?
>
> At death, you break up, the bits that were you
> Start speeding away from each other for ever
> . . . . .
> Not knowing how, not hearing who, the power
> Of choosing gone. Their looks show that they're for it:
> Ash hair, toad hands, prune face dried into lines –
> How can they ignore it?

The lines quoted from the first stanza seem like an outright attack on the helpless elderly, but the speaker's identification with them begins to emerge in its final question and is overt in the second stanza. The guiding pronoun shifts from "they" to "you," from the old fools to everyone. (There is even a "we" in a line I have elided.) At the same time, the poet's anger shifts onto nature, which disperses human remains according to its own fury. And the final question is more a plea than a denunciation.

Larkin's greatest success in the mordant mode is surely the ironically titled "Aubade," a cheerless dawn-song. It must be quoted in full:

> I work all day, and get half-drunk at night.
> Waking at four to soundless dark, I stare.
> In time the curtain-edges will grow light.
> Till then I see what's really always there:
> Unresting death, a whole day nearer now,
> Making all thought impossible but how
> And where and when I shall myself die.
> Arid interrogation: yet the dread
> Of dying, and being dead,
> Flashes afresh to hold and horrify.

The mind blanks at the glare. Not in remorse
 The good not done, the love not given, time
Torn off unused – nor wretchedly because
An only life can take so long to climb
Clear of its wrong beginnings, and may never;
But at the total emptiness for ever,
The sure extinction that we travel to
And shall be lost in always. Not to be here,
Not to be anywhere,
And soon; nothing more terrible, nothing more true.

This is a special way of being afraid
No trick dispels. Religion used to try,
That vast moth-eaten musical brocade
Created to pretend we never die,
And specious stuff that says *No rational being*
Can fear a thing it will not feel, not seeing
That this is what we fear – no sight, no sound,
No touch or taste or smell, nothing to think with,
Nothing to love or link with,
The anaesthetic from which none come round.

And so it stays just on the edge of vision,
A small unfocused blur, a standing chill
That slows each impulse down to indecision.
Most things may never happen: this one will,
And realisation of it rages out
In furnace-fear when we are caught without
People or drink. Courage is no good:
It means not scaring others. Being brave
Lets no one off the grave.
Death is no different whined at than withstood.

Slowly light strengthens, and the room takes shape.
It stands plain as a wardrobe, what we know,
Have always known, know that we can't escape,
Yet can't accept. One side will have to go.
Meanwhile telephones crouch, getting ready to ring.
In locked-up offices, and all the uncaring
Intricate rented world begins to rouse.
The sky is white as clay, with no sun.

Work has to be done.
Postmen like doctors go from house to house.

Everyone readily admits that death is inevitable but not so readily that the fear of death is inevitable. The middle stanza in particular exposes this fear as fundamentally irrational. It cannot be dispelled by courage, although that is one sanguine illusion. (Doubtless people of different temperaments are differently susceptible to the fear of death, but the poem only indirectly concerns itself with the matter of degree.)[21] Nor can it be reasoned away, rationalized, as sages from the time of the ancient Stoics and Epicureans to the present have tried to do. For it is rooted in the fact that being dead is unimaginable, that it baffles thought. And so we can't accept what we know we can't escape, an unresolvable dilemma.

In an essay titled "Joy or Night: Last Things in the Poetry of W. B. Yeats and Philip Larkin," Seamus Heaney compares the two poets and specifically the two poems "The Cold Heaven" and "Aubade" very decidedly to the latter's disadvantage.[22] Few would question that the scope and resource of Yeats's poetic energy is greater than Larkin's, but Heaney's comparison is nonetheless unsatisfactory.

His distaste for what he takes to be Larkin's defeatism leads him to judge the two poems moralistically. Heaney describes admirably the body of Yeats's poem as "a sudden apprehension that there is no hiding place" but makes a curious judgment about its conclusion. Although Yeats, as we saw, found no answer to its baffled and frustrated final question, for Heaney the poem "suggests that there is an overall purpose to life"; it implies the existence of a "circumambient energy and order within which we have our being." "The Cold Heaven" seems to me a more troubled and skeptical poem than this. But what I question is the way Heaney uses it as a stick to beat Larkin's more skeptical poem. Might not a poem of the later twentieth century decline to suggest "an overall purpose to life" yet still offer the kind of aesthetic satisfaction he himself values?

After quoting the whole of "Aubade," Heaney comments:

This, for me, is the definitive post-Christian English poem, one that abolishes the soul's traditional pretension to immortality and denies the Deity's immemorial attribute of infinite personal concern. Moreover, no matter how much or how little readers may at the outset be in sympathy with these views, they still arrive at the poem's conclusion a little surprised at how far it has carried them on the lip of its rhetorical wave. It leaves them like unwary surfers hung over a great emptiness, transported further into the void than they might have expected to go.

In context, this passage is clearly part of an indictment. "Aubade" is frigid, negative, terrified, defeatist (especially the line "Death is no different whined at than withstood"), and Heaney adds that Larkin, unlike Beckett, fails "to do something positive with bleakness," to show any "transformative way with language." He then rolls in for support Czeslaw Milosz's outright denunciation of the poem: " ['Aubade'] leaves me not only dissatisfied but indignant. . . . Death in the poem is endowed with the supreme authority of Law and universal necessity, while man is reduced to nothing. . . . But poetry by its very essence has always been on the side of life."

Milosz and Heaney do not see what I see, the poem's tough-minded and inventive way of dismantling the illusory belief that the fear of death can be evaded. It asks us for the *courage* to face *this* fact, and it exemplifies this courage by the remarkable skill, poise, and even elegance of its expression. (Each of those ten-line stanzas, for example, repeats an intricate rhyme scheme, ababccdeed, and identically varied line lengths.) And there is something else about the poem that might have impressed them if they had been able to read Motion's biography and learn that after Larkin had got as far as the penultimate stanza (concluding with the line that especially irritated Heaney), he stopped for five months, unsure how to proceed.[23] For in the last stanza, without retracting the poem's crucial insight, he does show us a way forward. Although the poem remains inspired by the dread that "Flashes afresh to hold and horrify," the poet realizes finally that people cannot live with such awareness constantly in the forefront of their minds. As day resumes and life goes on, we put the dilemma to the side and go about our business, albeit under a sky "white as clay." Postmen carry messages that must be answered, and so will carry us into a future, just as doctors carry messages that may lead us toward death. Admittedly, such "redress" may seem weak to those offended by seeing religion described as a "vast moth-eaten musical brocade."

Along with the mordant poem that attempts to dismantle illusion, Larkin excelled at one other kind, the poem that seems to replace fear of death with an underlying wish for death or, better, a wish for oblivion and the cessation of conflict.

"Wants" is one example, a poem in which the repeated first and last lines of the first little stanza ("Beyond all this, the wish to be alone") are replaced by the repeated first and last lines of the second ("Beneath it all, the desire of oblivion runs"). Another is "Here," which narrates in fine detail a drive at night from "rich industrial shadows" into an isolated landscape presumably in the north of England and concludes with a stanza that constitutes a quint-essential piece of Larkinesque lyricism, bestowing a strange, pure glow on images of negation. It begins with the line "Loneliness clarifies. Here silence stands." And it ends: "Here is unfenced existence; / Facing the sun, untalkative, out of reach." The poem makes eloquent the absence of people, sound, visibility, land, response of any kind. It is too delicate to accommo-date a heavy word like void, but some such idea is in the poet's mind. It attempts with imagery to capture something beyond imagery, changing the meaning of "here" into its perfect inversion: nowhere.

Probably Larkin's most important poem in this vein is "High Windows," partly because it offers some insight into what prompts the desire for oblivion.

> When I see a couple of kids
> And guess he's fucking her and she's
> Taking pills or wearing a diaphragm,
> I know this is paradise
>
> Everyone old has dreamed of all their lives –
> Bonds and gestures pushed to one side
> Like an outdated combine harvester,
> And everyone going down the long slide
>
> To happiness, endlessly. I wonder if
> Anyone looked at me, forty years back,
> And thought, *That'll be the life;*
> No God any more, or sweating in the dark
>
> About hell and that, or having to hide
> What you think of the priest. He
> And his lot will go down the long slide
> *Like free bloody birds*. And immediately
>
> Rather than words comes the thought of high windows:
> The sun-comprehending glass,
> Beyond it, the deep blue air, that shows
> Nothing, and is nowhere, and is endless.

The poem illustrates Larkin's masterly use of demotic speech giving way almost mysteriously to a quite different kind of diction. Where does the sudden "thought of high windows" come from and what does it mean? Until the final stanza, the poem deals with typical Larkinesque emotions—anger at frustrated desire, envy of the young—but the speaker seems to have tied his thinking into knots by inadvertently introducing a perspectival view of his situation. He wonders if he was once envied in his youth as he envies those who are now young. To see the matter in that way is to understand that he is basically *like* them, and this checks his anger and envy, which derived from feeling *unlike* them. The poet doesn't have to tell us this. He prefers to suggest that when crude emotion is submitted to reflection, it may find itself at an impasse. Realizing that he can neither act out nor renounce his desires, he seeks to escape conflict altogether through dissolution into undefined space. "The long slide" of sexual paradise, associated with the young and then with himself when young, is replaced in his mind by a different kind of endlessness whose content is "nothing" and "nowhere."

"When Larkin lifts his eyes from nature, what appears is a great absence. . . . Out there, no encounter is possible. Out there is not our business." Heaney's description of "High Windows" is not inaccurate, but I question its implication. Is a poet really out of sync with his age if he imagines an "out there" where no encounter is possible and that is not our business? I think Larkin has done something poetically impressive despite the bleakness. He has through language transformed the crude emotions of anger and envy into a difficult-to-achieve intimation of nothingness. He has given us a picture of mind imagining the end of mind.

Czeslaw Milosz: Modernist in Spite of Himself

In essays and poems, Milosz (1911–2004) acknowledged that the two principal influences on his view of the world have been his Catholic education and the Romanticism absorbed from his immersion in the language and literature of Poland. Together, they inspired him to mount and maintain, across a productive life of seventy years, a broad attack on modernism in general (the wasteland mentality, the avant-garde contempt for comprehensibility, and so on) and in particular on certain dangerous shapers of the modern mind. It is a somewhat old-fashioned attack, though not unattractive from a humanistic point of view.

His major villains are the scientific Weltanschauung, Rousseauism, and Friedrich Nietzsche—representing three kinds of arrogance that diminish human beings by diminishing their world. In *The Witness of Poetry*, Milosz tells us that the "lesson of biology," the knowledge that nature's total indifference to man changes him into a cipher, causes our imagination to lose its foundation, and, by removing the horizon of hope, is "aimed indirectly at the meaning of human death."[24] (A presumable example of this arrogance is Larkin's "Aubade.") In a poem called "Three Talks on Civilization," he refers to the second of his villains: "I detested these pups of foolish Jean-Jacques" because of their conceited "belief in their own noble nature."[25] As for Nietzsche's saying there is "no true world" (by which Milosz seems to have thought Nietzsche meant there is no material world rather than that every *belief* is a considering-something-true, hence relative to the believer), "Could we without perishing withstand a situation in which things surrounding us lose their being, where there is no true world?"[26] In sum, Milosz misses in the modern world the sense of a hopeful future for mankind, what he called, without obligatory metaphysical implication, "a sense of open space ahead of the individual and the human species."[27]

Among the writers whose work particularly attracted him were visionary poets from William Blake to Robinson Jeffers and several religious dialecticians whose vision might be described as severe: Blaise Pascal, Leo Shestov, and Simone Weil. Those names are a bit surprising because his work is different from theirs both in being more open to the world and more modest in demeanor.[28] But, though not attracted to theology as such, Milosz liked the idea of transcendence and welcomed the apocalyptic sweep he found in Blake and Jeffers as well as the purity of doubt and despair he found in Pascal, Shestov, and Weil. All of them helped to clear away skepticism and make room for what he sometimes called ecstasy. Given his prolonged and close exposure to the horrors perpetrated by Stalin and Hitler (Milosz was born in 1911 and did not leave Eastern for Western Europe, and thereafter America, until 1945), it is no surprise that he was dismayed by much in the modern world. But, because he was an idealist at heart, his pessimism tends to be admitted indirectly, as when he writes: "I prefer not to say that the earth is a madman's dream."[29] Again, "Poetry does not confirm the impression [that hope pervades our century], and it is a more reliable witness than journalism."[30]

Much of Milosz's attack on modernism now lacks bite. Take for example the view of science as hostile to the literary imagination. This is an idea that came in with the Romantics and has been kept alive by some later poets and by essayists who have feared (not without reason) the rapid advance of technology. But the literary situation has changed quite a lot since the 1960s, at least in America, as scores of new writers have been inspired *by* science. If we make some allowance for this, however, we find that what his Catholicism and Romanticism really amount to is a form of humanism. He values above all the dignity of man. Religion, he believes, helps to check arrogance and to maintain a sense of spaciousness in our lives, a sense of wonder and thankfulness that helps to prevent a soulless atheism. His main objection to the opinion of those who say there is no God is that others will be saddened by it![31]

As for Romanticism, a chapter called "A Quarrel with Classicism" in *The Witness of Poetry* indicates that this word means for him the willingness to break from precedent and convention in style and idea, hence "a passionate pursuit of the real." That is, Milosz does not align Romanticism with subjectivism but more nearly with its opposite. What may be called Romantic about his own style of modernism is mainly his desire to make his own cosmopolitan breadth of experience representative, and it is noteworthy in this respect that he regularly uses the names of various cities, from Poland to California, as subscripts to his poems.

Here is the Milosz Credo, stated not long after he won the Nobel Prize:

> To find my home in one sentence, concise as if hammered in metal. Not to enchant anybody. Not to earn a lasting name in posterity. An unnamed need for order, for rhythm, for form, which three words are opposed to chaos and nothingness.
> *Berkeley—Paris—Cambridge, Mass. (1981–1983)*[32]

It is a fascinating little statement. It turns aside from prophetic ambition and embraces an aesthetic ideal that opposes—not by an act of confrontation but simply by its presence—"chaos and nothingness." So here too we have a third-phase voice against the void. To be sure, Milosz tries to enlist his aesthetic ideal to support his philosophically naive quarrel with Nietzsche, writing that "the very act of naming things presupposes a faith in their existence and thus in a true world."[33] But this does not vitiate the modernist impulse behind his imagining of the end of life.

In the handful of poems he wrote about death, Milosz differs from his contemporaries mainly in speaking to the reader in a general as well as personal way. Even though these poems include self-reference, their imagery is more suggestive of worldly breadth than of psychological depth. After introducing a broad vista, they go on, like most that we have discussed in this chapter, to dramatize a shrinkage of consciousness toward point zero. They are of their age also in being incurious about death itself. They do not seek to confront it or look around it, as do the poems considered in the previous two chapters.

I should preface my comments on two of these poems by acknowledging that Milosz is the only one of the poets being considered in this or the last chapter who writes in a foreign language and one I do not understand. But nearly all of his poems, including "The Fall" and "Eyes" to be quoted below, have been co-translated by Milosz himself and so can make some claim to being English as well as Polish poems. Moreover, they (and many other Polish poems) read rather better in English than do many other translated poems, probably because they typically employ direct statement and a straightforward logic. Here, for example, is "The Fall":

> The death of a man is like the fall of a mighty nation
> That had valiant armies, captains, and prophets,
> And wealthy ports and ships over all the seas,
> But now it will not relieve any besieged city,
> It will not enter into any alliance,
> Because its cities are empty, its population dispersed,
> Its land once bringing harvest is overgrown with thistles,
> Its mission forgotten, its language lost,
> The dialect of a village high upon inaccessible mountains.
>   *Berkeley (1975)*[34]

No indication is given in this poem that the man in question was important or prominent in some way. He had the dignity of a human being and that is sufficient. His fall is nonetheless large-scaled and significant. The whole poem develops from that opening simile, comparing the fall of a man to the fall of a mighty nation. The five subsequent pronouns guiding the simile along through the rest of the poem all refer to the nation, not the man. Piece by piece the nation loses its valiant and honorable parts: armies, captains, prophets, ports, ships, cities, harvest, mission, and finally language itself. The impression we get until the last few lines is of a warrior-nation that has maintained itself honorably according to a warrior code—relieving besieged cities, entering into alliances. But in the last lines the fall becomes more poignant, with people dispersed and the harvest destroyed. Milosz saves what for him is apparently the keenest loss until the end, the loss of language itself, and the loss is keener because it involves not merely the brutal suppression of a language but also, in consequence, its virtual inaccessibility. It has become "The dialect of a village high upon inaccessible mountains." This is the poem's best and most moving line, alluding without self-pity to the emigrant poet's distance from the native language he loved and continued to use, although the poet had to make ever more room for a foreign language.[35] The "death" of the opening line is really the loss of identity, but it entails images appropriate to physical death as well, images that describe an irrevocable stripping away.

The second poem I will comment on, titled "Eyes," was first published in 2002 when Milosz was ninety-one years old,[36] and its theme of loss does certainly refer to the human body, and to the frailty of one of its prime faculties:

> My most honorable eyes. You are not in the best shape.
> I receive from you an image less than sharp,
> And if a color, then it's dimmed.
> And you were a pack of royal hounds
> With whom I would set forth in the early morning.
> My wondrously quick eyes, you saw many things,
> Countries and cities. Islands and oceans.
> Together we greeted immense sunrises,
> When the fresh air invited us to run
> Along trails just dry from cold night dew.
> Now what you have seen is hidden inside
> And changed into memory or dreams.
> Slowly I move away from the fair of this world
> And I notice in myself a distaste
> For monkeyish dress, shrieks, and drumbeats.
> What a relief. Alone with my meditation
> On the basic similarity of humans
> And their tiny grain of dissimilarity.
> Without eyes, my gaze is fixed on one bright point
> That grows large and takes me in.

The poet addresses his failing sight with no disgust and with barely perceptible dismay. His "eyes" are mocked gently, with soft touches of overstatement and understatement—they are "most honorable," "not in the best shape," "less than sharp." The emphasis soon shifts to the glorious days past when the "eyes," imagined as companions to the speaker rather than merely one of his faculties, are invoked as heroic, Odyssean: "My wondrously quick eyes, you saw many things, / Countries and cities. Islands and oceans. / Together we greeted immense sunrises." Then dismay is allowed to step forward, but it is really more like regret, and not even quite that since the past is retained in "memory or dreams." Yes, it goes on to say, "Slowly I move away from the fair of this world." But that retreat from pleasure is partly a welcome relief because it is a retreat also from what the senses now perceive as distasteful. Moreover, the speaker's thoughts in his restricted world are cheerful as well as thankful, finding that the "basic similarity of humans" outweighs "their tiny grain of dissimilarity."

It is only in the subtle last two lines, when the logic of the poem requires Milosz to confront what Larkin called "the only end of age," that his credentials as a contemporary imaginer of the end of life become apparent. There is no suggestion here that the moment will lead on to anything (heavenly, hellish, or purgatorial) or that it is in itself of spiritual importance. As in Dickinson's "I heard a Fly buzz — when I died," we find the image of light reduced to one bright point, but the poet shows little interest in creating from this a dramatic effect. The inward eye focuses on "a point / That grows large and takes me in." "Takes me in," if the context supported the implication, could suggest a providential consolation of some kind or could suggest, ironically, a deception of some kind. But in this case it is merely a blanched nothingness that is absorbing the speaker's nothingness. It marks, in other words, an end of differentiation, no more, no less. This imagery of canceling-out is much closer in spirit to what we find in Anthony's Hecht's poem "The Darkness and the Light," to be discussed soon, than what we found in earlier poems about the fading of the light of life.

I am not suggesting that Milosz is trying in this or any of his poems to imply the uselessness of religious faith. He remained an advocate of religion, if only formally a believer. But its value for him lay mainly in the fact that it could enhance the quality of life, could provide what he nicely called a "Second Space" (the title he chose for a volume of poems that would be published soon after his death). He did not appeal to religion for consolation at the hour of our death. Imaginatively he too leaned against the void, quietly accepting the meaninglessness of an afterlife as part of modern poetic consciousness. As he tells us in an autobiographical essay, while formally subscribing to the Gospels, "I must add immediately that when I think of my own death . . . I am no different from others and my imagination is rendered powerless just as theirs is."[37]

Denise Levertov's "Book Without Words"

The poetic voice of Denise Levertov (1923–97) is distinguished by its taut immediacy and emotional directness. Her subject might be the hidden wonder in nature, books, and human relationships; the tenderness and pain of love; lapses of inspiration; the destruction of life, a subject that gained prominence during the Vietnam War era and is central to the poem that this essay highlights; or aspects of sacred literature, a growing interest during her last decade. The voice is always that of a positive personality, and her presence had the same quality in the eyes of those who knew her.[38]

The precise and intent style Levertov forged for herself is modeled primarily on that of William Carlos Williams.[39] Her lines are generally short, often with space breaks after units of several lines, without rhyme or regular meter but canny in the use of pause, repetition, and pacing so that cliché, either of rhythm or phrase, is avoided and the reader is kept alert. In framing an aesthetic, her chief mentors were Keats, admired for his ability to feel his way into things, and Rilke, who combined with a comparable empathetic ability an interest in the dead.

Levertov's urgent poetic arguments do not seek compromise but are also disciplined enough to make intelligent qualifications. One poem evokes as "secret communion" the childhood experience of learning the name of a flower but knows that this experience is "once-in-a-lifetime." Another expresses the speaker's awed wonder at seeing forest elders rising "so far above me into the light" but acknowledges the transience of ecstasy. And one more affirms that "with each word [St. Augustine] set down . . . a skylight opened," while admitting that welcoming God is a difficult business.[40] Even in the angrier work of her middle period, the poet knows how to intensify rhetorical effect through stylistic restraint.

Levertov is perhaps the most religious of the poets considered in this chapter. Stevens and Bishop are politely aloof in regard to religious belief; Larkin is more or less critical; Milosz, although he misses in modern life the contribution belief might have made toward curbing pride and enhancing mutual respect (and was admired by Levertov for promoting "a culture of belief")[41] is not particularly drawn to its doctrine or vocabulary; and Hecht and Graham tend to see religion through the lens of literature. But we must put her commitment to religion in perspective. After 1984, Levertov did undergo a religious conversion but then defined herself as a "not very orthodox" Christian.[42] She had always been interested in the spiritual aspect of perceptual experience, and increasingly she was drawn to the poetic resonance of sacred literature. Moreover, she made poetic use of loyalty to parents who themselves were passionate about religion.[43] But, though her work has been described as neo-Romantic, its view of death closely resembles that of her contemporaries. And in particular, the poem I will focus on in this segment, "The Book Without Words," is a strong and original evocation of "the meaningless void."

Levertov's attachment to her parents should be pursued a little at this point because it is useful background for reading "The Book Without Words." The biographical sketch provided by Paul Lacey readily indicates its importance:

> She was born in Ilford, Essex, near London to a Welsh Congregationalist mother and a father who was Russian, a Hasidic Jew who had become a Christian and an Anglican priest. She and Olga, nine years her elder, were educated at home, in an atmosphere both intensely intellectual and deeply spiritual, at once cosmopolitan and tightly inward and enclosed. Both parents were scholarly. Her father wrote extensively on Jewish mysticism and the connections between Judaism and Christianity. He was a passionate, eloquent preacher. Both girls were intellectually precocious and encouraged to be old beyond their years. The parents entertained serious scholars, theologians and artists, and welcomed many refugees from Nazism into their home, and the girls were always drawn into their company.[44]

Given this background, it is not surprising that the emotional bond between her and her parents remained strong and positive or that it continued to influence her work.

In a late poem, she wrote, with reference to her father: "Along the way, / I have come to believe / the truth of what you believe."[45] One of the most moving of Levertov's parent-poems is "Enduring Love," giving us a snapshot of remembered loved ones rich in sentiment but without sentimentality. It describes "the way / as they climbed the steps / they appeared bit by bit," and then "their short stature / and their complete / comforting embrace."[46] Almost as moving, and more haunting as well as bolder in conception, is a poem called "The Change," containing these striking lines:

> And then they begin to return, the dead:
> but not as visions. They're not
> separate now, not to be seen, no,
> it's they who see: they displace,
> for seconds, for minutes, maybe longer,
> the mourner's gaze with their own.[47]

We perceive the influence of Rilke in these lines. Gazing at mourned parents in the mind's eye is not an uncommon experience, but this poem is seeking something more intense, the displacement of the gaze from the mourner to the dead who are mourned. *They* gaze at *us*, not because we are hallucinating

The Book (Das Buch), by Anselm Kiefer. Photo: Lee Stalsworth. Reproduced courtesy of the Hirshhorn Museum and Sculpture Garden, Smithsonian Institution, Thomas M. Evans, Jerome L. Greene, Joseph H. Hirshhorn, and Sydney and Frances Lewis Purchase Fund, 1985.

but because love remembered is strong enough to create an imaginative transfer of agency to the dead, "for seconds, for minutes, maybe longer."

For the purpose of reading "The Book Without Words" (published in 1989), it is especially important to cite the first few lines of "September 1961," written soon after her parents' death:

> This is the year the old ones
> the old great ones
> leave us alone on the road.

> The road leads to the sea.
> We have the words in our pockets,
> obscure directions. . . .[48]

The image of canceled communication and in particular the phrase "obscure directions" are revived with striking effect twenty-eight years later.

"The Book Without Words" is an ekphrastic poem, a work of literary art whose ostensible subject is a work of visual art. (A familiar instance is Auden's "Musée des Beaux Arts," based on Brueghel's painting *The Fall of Icarus*.) The painting involved in this case is Anselm Kiefer's *Das Buch* (1979–85). The poem was not included in her *Selected Poems*, perhaps because it entailed the problem of including a reproduction of the painting.[49] But since it is important for my purposes, I have taken the trouble to include one. (See photo on page 120.) The poem goes like this:

The Book Without Words
(From a painting by Anselm Kiefer)

The grey waves gnash
their teeth of foam.

Behind this verge,
the barren plain,
seamed, fissured.

Ahead, limitless ocean.
The sky's low ceiling
bears down upon it,
dark and darkening.

Here at the end of land
(not earth but cinders)

was to have been given
the ultimate direction.
The sea voyage was to begin.

And indeed the book
is here, a huge volume,
open and upright –
it levitates, close to the hiss of spume,

immutable, desolate, cast
in lead. Wordless.
If with great force its pages
were made to turn,
they would knock, unresonant,

one on another,
void upon void.
You have come to the shore.
There are no instructions.

Kiefer's painting, 10 1/2 feet high and 18 feet wide, is made from acrylic emulsion and shellac on canvas. The open book that is represented in the middle of the canvas—and placed near the shore where the barren plain is about to give way to the gnashing waves—is made of lead. (In other paintings, Kiefer makes use of thin and extensive rolled sheets of lead, and indeed this is one of his signatures.) The fissured and desolate, even cinderlike, aspect of the land is achieved by a patternless and roughened mix of whitish and darker colors including little strawlike thrusts. The land is hardly distinct from the sea, but one perceives toward the top of the painting what Levertov means by writing of the gnashing waves. "Limitless ocean" can only be imagined, but the "sky's low ceiling / bear[ing] down upon it" is surely the effect created by that ominously colored band across the top. The most dramatic feature of the painting is of course the lead book raised from the surface of the canvas so that it seems almost suspended above it rather than lying upon it. Its pages are very faintly darkened as if with print so that one strains to make out any markings but cannot do so. One hopes to find in the book some kind of direction or instruction, but all is "unresonant." Its pages, if they could be turned, would yield "void upon void."

Levertov further animates Kiefer's work by imagining a "you," an everyman, come to the shore as if to set forth on a voyage. The land behind is forbidding ("not earth but cinders"), and the sea ahead is forbidding as well—"teeth of foam," "darkening" sky, "hiss of spume." This is no primordial sea suggestive of birth or rebirth. It suggests only vacancy. Shouldn't there be some direction at such a juncture? We remember "September 1961," the poem about the emptiness created by the death of parents and particularly the lines: "The road leads to the sea. / We have the words in our pockets, / obscure directions." Alluding to this poem, the poet writes now that "the ultimate direction" "was to have been given," a canny use of passive voice that despairs of agency, human or divine. The ultimate direction is no longer even obscure but absent: "You have come to the shore. / There are no instructions." To the resonance of this allusion there is added our sense of the holocaust hovering in the background of both Kiefer's painting and Levertov's poem. Kiefer makes much use of holocaust imagery in his work (some have said too much), and Levertov, given her upbringing that included so much talk of Jews and Nazis among people with whom she identified profoundly, must have responded to this.[50] The Jews are sometimes called the people of the book, and I suspect that both poet and painter were drawn to the image of an empty book partly for this reason.[51]

There is something else too, something that excites my interest in the particular imagery characteristic of "third phase" post-Enlightenment poetry imagining the end of life. A book is the very emblem of meaning, of communication by means of words across time and space, on which we depend to find *some* instruction, *some* way forward. We have seen how other contemporary poets in effect cancel the consolatory use of images traditionally associated with death. Could one perhaps cancel the image of meaning itself? Well, yes and no. It is impossible to write a poem (though not impossible to paint a painting) without the use of words. But by filtering one's vision through a strong visual representation of an empty book, one can come daringly close. One can use words to void words. A critic must admire not only the skill but also the strength of mind required to bring this paradox to poetic life.[52]

Anthony Hecht: The Darkness and the Light

Hecht is a learnedly allusive, witty, and formally elegant poet. He has also written substantial volumes of literary criticism, among them *On the Laws of the Poetic Art* and *Melodies Unheard: Essays on the Mysteries of Poetry*, which are notable for the probing and subtle connections they make between poetry's formal character and its currents of feeling.

A sardonic and satiric tone is characteristic of his poems, as is the more subtle and suggestive kind of irony achieved by the speaker's distance from their emotive current. But that current, often dark and disturbed, is always palpable. A certain ominousness hangs about and around many of these poems, explicitly in the opening triad of "Nocturne: A Recurring Dream": "The moon is a pearl in mist and sets the scene. / Comfort seems within reach, just over there, / But rocks, water and darkness intervene."[53]

As a rule, the formal elegance and poise of a Hecht poem exist *in tension with* its ominous implications, as if holding them at bay. The epigraph prefacing "Venetian Vespers" and drawn from *Othello* makes a theme of this: "where's that palace whereunto foul things / Sometimes intrude not?" The foul things are usually distanced in some way, framed as in a picture. In "An Overview," the earth seen from an airplane resembles a large toy store, but, unlike "the Air Force boys" and the politicos, the imaginative speaker sees "in the toy store, right up close, / Chipped paint and mucilage represent / The wounded, orphaned, indigent, / The dying and the comatose." Often the foulness involves the memory of Nazi Germany, but this is accessed *indirectly*. In "More Light! More Light!" the tortured victim is a courageous *Pole* who refuses to kill Jews. In "Haman," Nazism is conveyed by the voice of the biblical Esther's enemy. "Still Life" engages a memory of being a soldier in Germany in the first light of dawn *before* the action of the day has begun. In "Sacrifice," the narrative of an escaping German soldier about to kill a French family that have concealed their bicycle is paralleled to the narrative of Abraham and Isaac about to kill and be killed, and the action in both narratives (as it was in "Still Life") is suspended so as to leave dark consequence unstated. In sum, for Hecht the interest of an emotionally charged *picture* takes precedence over whatever moral and psychological questions the poems might raise. We will return to this aspect of his art.

Both the initiating moment and chief direction of Hecht's poetic enterprise can, I believe, be located in a passage from the meditative blank verse poem titled "Apprehensions," published in *Millions of Strange Shadows*. The passage describes with unusual directness a cold and difficult childhood, but the poem is exceptional not simply as confession but as revelation of the moment the speaker discovers himself to be a poet, able through poetry to liberate himself from desolation by aestheticizing ordinary experience. "Apprehensions" begins by referring to "a grave and secret malady of my brother's" and to "various grown-up shames," circumstances that leave the seven-year-old subject to his own devices, "Except for a Teutonic governess / Replete with the curious thumb-print of her race / That special relish for inflicted pain." A multivolume *Book of Knowledge* becomes a treasure to the boy, and then we get this full picture of what must be called a conversion experience:

>   We were living at this time in New York City
> On the sixth floor of an apartment house
> On Lexington, which still had streetcar tracks.
> It was afternoon in the late summer;
> The windows were open; wrought-iron window guards
> Meant to keep pets and children from falling out.
> I, at the window, studiously watching
> A marvelous transformation of the sky;
> A storm was coming up by dark gradations.
> But what was curious about this was
> That as the sky seemed to be taking on
> An ashy blankness, behind which there lay
> Tonalities of lilac and dusty rose
> Tarnishing now to something more than dusk,
> Crepuscular and funerary grays,
> The streets became more luminous, the world
> Glinted and shone with an uncanny freshness.
> The brickwork of the house across the street

(A grim, run-down Victorian chateau)
Became distinct and legible; the air,
Full of excited imminence, stood still.
The streetcar tracks gleamed like the path of snails.
And all of this made me superbly happy,
But most of all a yellow Checker Cab
Parked at the corner. Something in the light
Was making this the yellowest thing on earth.
It was as if Adam, having completed
Naming the animals, had started
On colors, and had found his primary pigment
Here, in a taxi cab, on Eighty-ninth street.

The poet-to-be has begun to discover a way out of his cold world, not by means of some fortunate intervention from outside but by absorbing himself in the drama of a perceptual contrast between the darkening air and the bright yellow taxi, a drama played out for him (to adapt a line from Stevens) merely in living as and where he lives. The speaker will remind us that no immediate liberation has been achieved. Toward the poem's end we learn that the brother has been diagnosed with epilepsy, and at its end we learn that the speaker continues to dream of the ominous governess welcoming him home in fake-innocent German. But the perceptual experience proves unforgettable and endlessly generative.

"Venetian Vespers," written two years later, enhances the meaning of this incident. It acknowledges first that the "departure point" of the poet's experience of life has been "those first precocious hints of hell, / Those intuitions of living desolation / That last a lifetime." And it shows the way to a cure in these lines:

What is our happiest, most cherished dream
Of paradise? Not harps and fugues and feathers
But rather arrested action, an escape
From time, from history, from evolution
Into the blessed stasis of a painting.

A fair number of Hecht's poems are quite painterly in the way they arrest a narrative action by focusing intently on a climactic moment, without pursuing cause or consequence, as we would expect narrative to do. I have already mentioned several in this connection. "The Road to Damascus," "Still Life," and "Poppy" are equally illustrative. More remarkable are the fairly numerous poems that seek to achieve a painterly stasis by *chiar-*

oscuro, poems that describe a human situation in terms of a patterned balancing of light and dark, using *chiaroscuro* as an objective correlative for the emotional content of a poem. Among these are "Third Avenue in Sunlight," "A Cast of Light," "Late Afternoon: The Onslaught of Love," "Memory," "Mirror," "A Certain Slant," "Despair," "The Rainstorm," "Nocturne: A Recurring Dream," "The Ashen Light of Dawn," and the one I want to highlight in this essay, perhaps the subtlest and richest of the group despite its brevity, "The Darkness and the Light Are Both Alike to Thee." Behind all of them stands Dickinson's "There's a certain slant of light." Dickinson's slant of light induces the "hurt" of "Despair," but it is "Heavenly hurt" and points to "Where the meanings are," much as in Hecht's "Mirror" the "shade of gray" on "winter afternoons" points to "Those shrouded regions where the meanings are."

Given Hecht's tendency to aestheticize experience and look indirectly at harsh subject matter, it is not surprising that he approaches the subject of death with some irony. Sometimes indeed the irony is too pat, as in a sequence of poems headed "The Presumptions of Death" (from the volume titled *Flight from the Tombs*), eliciting from us a weak smile. We get, for example, "Death Demure" shyly waiting to speak until "all's said and done"; "Death the Inquisitor" affirming "There is no match for my patience"; "Death the Judge" calm and unbiased as he hands out the "predetermined sentence"; "Death the Film Director" proud to have designed "an inevitable plot." The most complex of these is "Death the Whore," but that is because it eschews the superficially macabre tone of the others and explores instead the disappointments of desire.

But after Hecht himself turned seventy and faced the prospect of death more nearly and personally, he wrote several poems, placed at the end of *The Darkness and the Light,* that touch on the subject of aging and death with a more subtle and sensitive kind of indirection, more sensitive in that they introduce a measure of tenderness, a quality not much in evidence elsewhere in the oeuvre.[54] One of these, "I.M.E.M.," is a little tribute to the quiet courage of a dying friend who committed suicide. Another is "Sarabande on Attaining the Age of Seventy-seven." The diminishment that comes with age is presented here through the metaphor of a graceful and stately dance. It concludes:

A turn, a glide, a quarter-turn and bow,
The stately dance advances; these are airs
Bone-deep and numbing as I should know by now,
Diminishing the cast, like musical chairs.

There is a touch of grimness in the phrase "Bone-deep and numbing," but this modulates into the resigned acceptance of "as I should know by now" and, in the last line, slides gently back into the metaphor of the dance, as if the dance itself rather than the speaker is gradually winding down.

I want to devote the rest of this little essay to an analysis of the third and last poem of the group:

"The Darkness and the Light Are Both Alike to Thee"

Psalms 139:12
Like trailing silks, the light
Hangs in the olive trees
As the pale wine of day
Drains to its very lees:
Huge presences of gray
Rise up, and then it's night.

Distantly lights go on.
Scattered like fallen sparks
Bedded in peat, they seem
Set in the plushest darks
Until a timid gleam
Of matins turns them wan,

Like the elderly and frail
Who've lasted through the night,
Cold brows and silent lips,
For whom the rising light
Entails their own eclipse,
Brightening as they fail.

The most fruitful point of departure for an analysis of this poem is the title-phrase and the wonderful psalm from which it is drawn. Here are the psalmist's verses leading up to and including the one cited by Hecht: "If I take the wings of the morning and dwell in the uttermost parts of the sea; even there shall thy hand lead me, and thy right hand shall hold me. If I say, Surely the darkness shall cover me, even the night shall be light about me. Yea, the darkness hideth not from thee; but the night shineth as the day; the darkness and the light are both alike to thee." What interests Hecht about the verse he cites is not man's faith in the Lord's protectiveness as expressed in the fuller citation but something else that cannot be quickly paraphrased.

Commenting on this poem and this psalm in a newspaper interview about the publication of *The Darkness and the Light,* Hecht said that the psalm is about "the divine indifference to good fortune and bad. . . . Darkness and light seem like antitheses, but for the divine being they are the same."[55] By "divine indifference" he meant to indicate not any sort of failing as we understand failing but, rather, the divine being's incommensurable superiority to human understanding. The Lord possesses knowledge "too wonderful for me; it is high, I cannot attain unto it." Yet this is not a poem about our awe and wonder before God or about our relation to God in any way. It is a poem that develops a parallel between the morally neutral sublimity of the Lord and the morally neutral aesthetic stance of the poet for whom the distinction between life and death is expressed in terms of a balancing between light and dark, dark and light. *The Darkness and the Light* as a volume is introduced by two epigraphs: "Aye, on the shores of darkness there is light" (John Keats); and "The exceeding brightness of this early sun / Makes me conceive how dark I have become" (Wallace Stevens). As a rule, dual epigraphs are congruent in meaning, but here they are antithetical, which, I am suggesting, is Hecht's way of indicating that contrast is more interesting for him formally than semantically or symbolically.

I am not suggesting that Anthony Hecht seeks to distance himself from the Bible, Judaism, or religion. He seems to find all of these congenial, but his loyalty to them tends to be expressed diffidently.[56] (The nearest he comes to worrying about Judaism is a searching essay on *The Merchant of Venice,* in *Obbligati: Essays in Criticism,* in which he shows, by way of aligning Shylock with the devil-figure, that the Law/Old Testament versus Love/New Testament distinction used by critics is untrue both to the play and to the Bible.) What his poetry shows is that the moral dimension of experience is absorbed by the aesthetic dimension.

"The Darkness and the Light" is remarkably impersonal, despite its intimate tonality. The first two of its three stanzas make no reference to a human situation. The first describes the light hanging, the day fading, and the darkness rising. The draining of wine to the lees is a human act, but it is described here as the act of "day." "Presences" has an anthropomorphic connotation, but here it refers only to a color, "gray." The second stanza describes lights coming on at night. We know human beings have turned them on, but our attention is focused only on the lights themselves, on what they look like in the darkness ("scattered like fallen sparks," "bedded in peat," "set in the plushest darks"). Finally they turn "wan" as morning arrives, without any mention of the fact that human beings turn them off.

The third stanza is the most cunning in its impersonality. It does, to be sure, refer to a human situation and an emotionally charged one (the elderly and frail who last through the night), but it seems to contain no grammatical subject. In the last line, at last, there is a "they," but it is difficult to see that this must refer to "the elderly and frail" because there are four nouns between this phrase and the pronoun and because the phrase is really the object of a preposition rather than the subject of a clause. The phrase, via the pronominal "who" (in who've), becomes the subject of a clause, but the whole stanza is syntactically peculiar. It is all the more so because it is connected to the second stanza by a comma, so that the "they" seems to refer as well to the dominant noun "lights," which in the course of that stanza do in some sense "fail" (that is, turn "wan").

This is not careless writing on Hecht's part but a (perhaps excessively) subtle way of contrasting the rising light of morning to the eclipsing light of the elderly persons. It also parallels that contrast to the reverse relationship between the falling light of day and the man-caused, rising light of night. In the interview noted earlier, Hecht remarked that he had written the first stanza ten years before he saw how to continue and conclude the poem. When he found a way to do so, he introduced an element of human interest, "the elderly and frail." But this phrase is only part of a simile, and the "eclipse" of these persons has less to do with the traditional symbolic association of darkness with death and light with life than with the parallel between one kind of natural rising light and another kind of natural failing light.

The elderly and frail are soon to enter into the darkness of death. The poem takes that for granted and makes use of the fact. Hecht is too concrete a poet to write of "the void," but he is of his time in writing about nearing death rather than about looking beyond it or outfacing it in some way. He is of his time, above all, in not seeking consolation, yet in finding a music that substitutes for it.

It is fair to say that in this poem formal symmetry interests Hecht particularly. The rhyme scheme, for example, is an intricate abcbca pattern, two enclosed repetitions within one frame repetition. But the wonder of the poem is that it is not as cold as we might therefore expect. In some way, no doubt a trick of rhythm and diction as well as rhyme, Hecht has been able to make formal elegance support and even enhance a funereal music; he has been able to elicit the mood of dwindling down without arousing the pathos inherent in such a mood. Trying to explain this effect to myself, I called to mind two comments Hecht himself made in his critical writings. One is about Milton's "Lycidas." Referring to Samuel Johnson's opinion that because of its artifice Milton's elegy expresses no real grief, Hecht wrote, "that has not in the least diminished the beauty, the grandeur, or the deep funereal music of that poem."[57] The other comment concerns a poem by Housman. Hecht wrote that Housman's "metrical and musical powers have enchained [his poem, 'He stood and heard the steeple'] with a chilling closure and finality."[58]

Jorie Graham: Void and Eloquence

Graham is a difficult poet, as in a similar way are her chief predecessors, Wallace Stevens and John Ashbery. All of them lead their critics toward a higher level of abstraction and a lower level of interpretive confidence than some are quite comfortable with. But I give her work final consideration in this survey because what it tells us about the meaning (or meaninglessness) of "void" in contemporary poetry is not only illuminating but also provides a full stop to the argument I have been developing in these pages.

Graham's titles, although often ironic (like those that feature the words "Aubade" or "Guardian Angel" or "Prayer"), usually give us a helpful clue to a poem's meaning. Perhaps the most helpful ones for clarifying the general drift of her work are *The Dream of the Unified Field* (the main title of *Selected Poems: 1974–1991*) and *The Errancy* (the title of the successive volume).

"Dream" for this poet denotes both the persisting desire to find coherence and stability in the ambient world and the illusion that this desire can be satisfied. She is centrally concerned with change, less with historical, psychological, or biological change (conspicuous themes of many other poets) than with the phenomenology of change in the world that presents itself to our consciousness, a concern captured in one title phrase: "Of the Ever-Changing Agitation in the Air." In using the word "errancy," Graham is calling attention to the idea that not only the physical world but also desire or consciousness itself is always agitated so that its responses are those of a "seriously wounded narrator," a phrase borrowed by her in "Desert/Dune" from the critic Hélène Cixous.[59] She is fascinated by "the gaze" (a phrase picked up from feminist literary criticism and from a Dickinson poem rather than from Jacques Lacan, who made it fashionable) because it underscores her belief that we see others through a filter of needy desire and that our view of the world is therefore likely to be errant. We "dream of reason" ("The Scanning") as we dream of perfect patterning ("The Guardian Angel of the Little Utopia"). Yet, however errant, desire is to be taken seriously. It is rooted in the body and imperative in its need. It seeks to dent and be dented by the world, especially where lovers are involved, but the bodies of lovers (as in "The Strangers") are like the blossoms of flowers in "Over and Over Stitch," "pale and inconclusive utterances." The Thomas Wyatt line used as epigraph to *The Errancy*—"Since in a net I seek to hold the wind"— epitomizes the predicament. Nevertheless, the agitations of the air and of the desiring consciousness are ubiquitous and absolute. As the poem "Surf" puts it, "there is no plural of change . . . or thirst."[60]

The very first poem of *The Dream of the Unified Field*, "The Way Things Work," concludes with these lines:

I believe in you—
your head is the horizon to
my hand. I believe
forever in the hooks.
The way things work
is that eventually
something catches.

This reminds us of Whitman's "noiseless, patient spider" launching forth "filament, filament, filament, out of itself" until it "catch somewhere," an action the poet compares to that of his soul. But Graham's confidence in our ability to "catch somewhere" soon gave way, and her poems became concerned instead with the problem of not being able to do so.

Indeed they have become increasingly suspicious of the security we take for granted in using common words and phrases. Finding no stability either in smallness (since atoms are divisible) or magnitude ("A he referring to God may be capitalized or not"), the poet (in *Swarm*) then turns sharply upon innocent-seeming phrases, producing a collagelike arrangement on the page that is intelligible as philosophic anxiety. I have drawn from several of her poems (each titled "Underneath" followed by a different number) to make a composite that illustrates this device:

explain given to
explain born of
explain asks to be followed
explain remains to be seen
explain two are
explain not one
explain edges
explain duty to remain to the end.

The poem titled "Hunger" (in *Never*) makes a sort of game, in fact, of illogi-cal randomness. Having learned that every nine minutes a species of life becomes extinct and estimating that it takes about nine minutes to read one of her own poems, Graham writes a poem that looks like a group of succes-sive journal entries, its subheadings extending from 11:54 a.m. through 12:02 p.m.

Jorie Graham has devised a distinctive free-verse style—concisely de-scribed on the jacket of *Never* as "accretion, dilation, pause, leap"—to ren-der the effect of randomness. The poems are ordered neither by arrange-ments of meter and rhyme nor by logical and narrative progression. A sense of coherence and movement is gained by various forms of anaphora, espe-cially the lining up of participles or compound verbs, and by circling, irregu-larly, around a particular idea, image, or situation. This means that the actual lines of a Graham poem are usually too fluid to be memorable, although they are often witty about this very difficulty. A fascination with logical gaps and blanks is a risky affair, after all. It is impressive when it successfully expresses the effect of randomness while remaining intelligible.[61] But an imitation of confusion may sometimes result in confusion itself. Of course there may not be consensus as to whether a difficult passage is intelligible, but her poems have, in fact, become more bizarre in their punctuation and spacing and more densely mannered, giving us some strangely abrupt jux-tapositions as well as single sentences that contain brackets, parentheses, a dash or two, a colon, and blank space.

There is some evidence to suggest that Graham thinks of her poems as bearing a heavy tragic burden. The jacket copy of *Never* uses such weighty phrases as "acute moral bewilderment," "a ferocious urgency to describe the disappearing world," and "the pressure of history, representation and be-lief." In earlier poems especially, she dealt with such somber subject matter as the holocaust, rape, and children at risk. And there's no question that potentially dark subjects like mutability, illusion, and emptiness are among her major poetic themes. But the spirit of her work is not really anguished but mostly buoyant and spirited. It seems to me that evoking dismay and horror is not her real strength (and I think Graham herself has come to realize this, perhaps reluctantly). Her work might be best described as that of a philosophical ironist, more stimulated than appalled by perceptions of incongruity and unpredictability.[62]

Some supporting evidence for this characterization is worth attention at this point because it will assist my reading of the poem I want to examine closely, "Against Eloquence." A poem called "The Lovers" uses the phrase "the end of beauty," where "end" means not goal but result. The poem is not, as it seems at first, about disillusionment but about the lovers' experience of strangeness in realizing how little their own hope and expectation have brought about the present moment of their lives as they now perceive it.

> They have been staring at each other for a long time now.
> Around them the objects (circa 1980).
> Then corridors, windows, a meadow, the _____.
> They have been staring at the end of each other for a long
> time now.
> She tries to remember but it is hopeless. She tries the other one—
>   Hope—casting outward
> a bit.
> oh but it costs too much.
> Either they're coming for us now or they're not says Love.
> Around them objects, minutes, *No* said quickly in passing.
> Here it is, *here*, the end of beauty, the present.
> What the vista fed into.[63]

A second example is "The Guardian Angel of Self-Knowledge," a poem exposing the vanity—but still more the odd absurdity—of attempting to know oneself. It ends:

> who will they be when they get to the bottom of it,
> when they've stripped away the retrospect, when they've peeled
>   away the
> orphanhood, the shimmering merriments of consolation?
> How will they feel when the erasures erase them?
> Who will they resemble when they're done with resemblance?

This reduction of the traditional constituents of human identity arouses in us an inward smile rather than pity or dread.

And a third example is "The Guardian Angel of the Private Life," another witty poem, this time about trying to order one's life by making a "next day's list." Fussing about the *"integrity of the whole"* is an enterprise that is broken up, not from without but merely by the distracting abundance of random self-questioning. It ends with a simple imperative, referring to "this list you hold / in your exhausted hand": "Oh put it down." Such a conclusion excites in us almost a chuckle of relief as we escape from its net of words.

We are ready now for a reading of "Against Eloquence" from perhaps her best volume, *The Errancy*. A preliminary clue to the meaning of the poem will be useful. It is not the poet who is against eloquence but "the void." Eloquence of course includes language but here also all sorts of human activity, whatever we do to keep ourselves going. Our characteristic human effort, as the opening poem of *The Errancy* puts it, is "stuffing the void with eloquence."

Then there was the sense of a vectored landing – very
    fast.
We decided it was speed after all that could carry us.
We decided to decide. The drowse lifted. Something
    resembling air
glinted . Elsewhere a violin – alone – just done
    warming up,
the lovely sequencing beginning, stillness decomposing
where the notes rise up into it. And in the alcove two
    people in black
kissing a long time. And the frontier where the notes
    pulse, fringe, then fray
the very same stillness we place our outlines
in, the very same one we have to breathe, and flare our
    tiny nets of words
into (who's there?)(what do you hear?)(what hear?)
    (still
there?) – the very same – we listen in there –
the zero glistens – the comma holds –
flames behind where the siren goes off,
where someone is killed but only *by accident* so you
    you are free to cross the street now –
I watch the lovers a long time –
they kiss as if trying to massacre difference –
the alcove around them swarms its complex mechanism
    made to resemble emptiness –
the shoppers go by; some vacuum hums;
something unseen, under-used, tarnishes; the daffodils
endowed by the widow x flourish – the lovers gnaw
    – the lovers
want to extinguish something –

something I know how to kill with a word, a single
    word –
the violin roils across the square –
they fracture emptiness to tiny masks – put each
    one on –
here's *smile* – here's *clenched* –
here's *fear* – here's *more* – emptiness doesn't
    take notice –
downpour of architectural void doesn't disturb –
moderation of accumulative time,
vague fabric tossed over the fire
as if to squelch it, ripples in the heat –
daffodils enter the decomposition known as yellow-
edges of the patio pulse –
violin notes float, wrinkling, unwrinkling – no –
they are not wrinkled – the message not delivered
    – nothing
at the address now – notes rinsing nothing –
nothing bleached by their acid –
nothing illumined by the ten thousand red tulips –
by the caustic justice of such gleaming beds
    deployed by a city
to force a plaza. . . .
April. . . .
Now the lovers are burying their arsenal.
Now with their stillness they navigate as usual.
Don't you know it's upstream? Don't you know you are
    supposed to look?
Right at the place their mouths mark, the place
    their mouths puncture –
What is the void once it is forced to cross through
    fire?

A vector, one of Graham's favorite words and useful for her ironic purposes, is a quantity completely specified by a magnitude and a direction. The poem starts with a gesture of confidence and speed, but, although speed (or more exactly agitation) continues, confidence is quickly dissipated by the pseudopurposeful "decided to decide" and the series of seemingly random notations that make up the body of the poem.

Half a dozen different activities are specified in disorderly alternation, a cacophonous assault on air and emptiness (or on what resembles these, about which resembling more in a moment). A violin plays, lovers are kissing, a street accident has occurred involving flames and a siren, daffodils and tulips appear in April, and quietly in the background "shoppers go by; some vacuum hums / something unseen, under-used tarnishes." These actions look less benign as the poem proceeds. At first the violin warms up and sounds lovely—"stillness decomposing / where the notes rise up to it." Later it "roils across the square," and its notes "fracture emptiness." And at last its notes are like an undeliverable message, affecting "nothing." The lovers in an alcove at first kiss "a long time," then kiss "as if trying to massacre difference," then "gnaw," wanting "to extinguish something" before "burying their arsenal." The flames seem to be part of an accident causing a temporary street-detour, but someone is killed, the flames are not quite subdued, and the phrase "cross through fire" is placed in the emphatic terminal position of the poem. The flowers are at first noted as merely endowed by some widow, then they decompose, and "nothing [is] illumined" by them.

This mounting aggressiveness is important to the poem. The agents decompose, fracture, massacre, extinguish, bleach—what? The objects of assault are air, stillness, emptiness, difference, nothing, void. But Graham writes "something resembling air" and "made to resemble emptiness." Moreover, "emptiness doesn't take notice," "void doesn't disturb," "nothing [is] at the address." The agents of "Against Eloquence" appear to be urgent, anxious, and fearful about the object of their assault, as if this nothing is something, this void a force. They are stuffing the void with eloquence. But it is a major idea in Graham's world that the void is not a meaningful concept because matter is infinitely divisible. A later poem, "The Guardian Angel of the Swarm," makes the point explicitly: "The façade is riddled with holes, although there is no void / (a hole being only the site of a more rarefied matter) –."

Also important to a reading of the poem is making sense of the shift in grammatical person, although I find this shift at the end of the poem ambiguous. It begins with a "we," the poet positioning herself with the reader and the poem's specified agents. And she does so as a poet. The stillness into which the violin notes "pulse, fringe, then fray" is "The very same stillness we place our outlines / in, the very same one we have to breathe, and flare our tiny nets of words / into. . . . the very same – we listen in there." I take the next line—"the zero glistens – the comma holds"—to mean that any kind of eloquence we can summon to fight off erosion and death will make the world seem to gleam. For a poet in particular, a way of saying this is that "the comma holds"—that is, the flow of language is paced but not stopped. Like violinist or lover, says the poem, "I [too] know how to kill with a word, a single word." Yet in most of the poem "I" is positioned as a spectator of "they" and is implicitly critical of the latter's naiveté about the nature of the void. In the three long last lines, the positioning of grammatical person shifts again and is perhaps confusing. The poet addresses the lovers in the second person and then refers to them once more in the third person, and it is hard to tell whether she is identifying with their difficulty or berating them. In the inevitably important final line, the point of view is unspecified, but I am inclined to understand it as Graham speaking in her own person, telling us in an ironic way that there is no void, and that only our fear prompts us to believe that the void needs to be destroyed.

The title of the poem immediately following "Against Eloquence," "That Greater Than Which Nothing," seems to refer simultaneously to the allness of God and the void of Nothingness. "Greater Than Which Nothing Is" was a way of referring to God in medieval thought. By simply dropping "Is" and adding an initial, conjunctive "That," Graham suggests that Nothing occupies the same space as Allness. In the age of faith, this meant that God filled all. Today it means that random perceptions (what Ashbery called "pointless diversity") fills all instead. Since this pointless diversity could be understood as either a something or a nothing, one could also say that for Graham allness and nothingness, plenitude and void, are merely alternative descriptions of the same reality.

Writing poems about the void but not, like other poets in this study, about individual death, Jorie Graham helps us see that the two subjects present much the same problem to the imagination. We can think *about* our death, but we cannot imagine *being* dead and unable to think at all. The same is true of the so-called void. We fear the cessation of consciousness, and so we stuff the void with whatever kind of eloquence we can muster, making nothing into something. A meaningless void cannot be thought, and Graham exposes the illusion of thinking that it can be.

Eloquence is what we have—is all we have—in the face of void. It is our response to meaninglessness. To the creative consciousness, the prospect of the end of consciousness is fearful, but it is also an endless spur to invention, however different from past forms the current forms of that invention may be.

Conclusion

All the Dead Voices

I have been discussing three successive styles used by post-Enlightenment poets, faced with the loss of socially supported beliefs in an afterlife and its consolations, to imagine the end of life. To put it another way, I have been discussing three styles of resistance to the prospect and difficulty of feeling and thinking nothing. But if we stand back from the content and style of specific poems and consider the act of writing itself in the broad economy of life, we can say further that all writing is a kind of response to this prospect and this difficulty. We wish to leave words behind, more or less as we wish to leave children, bits of eloquence by means of which we hope to have our existence acknowledged beyond the hour of our death.

From this standing-back position, there is another aspect of the relation between writing and death that comes to the fore. In a profound though metaphorical sense, death is *always already* part of the writer's—and in turn of the reader's—enterprise. Postmodern philosophers have stressed this idea, and many modern poets, especially French poets, have done so as well. But their language is abstract, and in these concluding remarks I would like to spell out this important adjunctive idea in my own vocabulary.

We sometimes call writing an act of self-expression, meaning that a portion of the writer's identity or consciousness is transferred onto paper in the form of words. Many writers have testified that they experience this transfer as a separation, a loss, a kind of death—despite the pride they may feel in their work and the practical advantages that accrue from accomplishing it. Writers sometimes speak in this connection of postparturitional depression, and do so in spite of the fact that they know from experience that they are likely to be made "pregnant" again.

As for writing itself apart from the writer, it traces a contrary course, not from life to death but from death to a new kind of life. Words on the page by themselves are inert, unliving things, unless and until they are reanimated by the responsive consciousness of readers. Thinking about the peculiar ontological status of printed words, the vitalist D. H. Lawrence spoke of them as not life but tremulations upon the ether. Never mind the now obsolete notion of ether—"tremulations" captures nicely this ambiguous status.

We may fairly think of writing as a protest against death rather than a denial of it. For a knowing resistance to death is an admission of its reality. Writers contrast sharply in this respect to many political and military leaders who justify the killing of others by denying their status as living human beings like themselves—calling them, for example, "evil terrorists," "barbarians," *Figuren* (puppets, as the Nazis called the dead Jews in their camps), and "cockroaches" (as the Hutus called the Tutsis). No doubt writers may also lie to themselves, but they stand a better chance of becoming authentic human beings in the Heideggerian sense, people who live intimately with the knowledge of their own finitude, their own being toward death.

Readers may be said to undergo an experience similar to that of writers, for, by lending themselves to what they read, they bring back to "life" the "dead" words on the page. This renovative aesthetic experience is inevitably temporary, to be sure, for when it subsides, the words become inert again. But readers can then repeat the experience and not once but many times. And there is a further peculiarity concerning the experience of reading. Even after the aesthetic response has lost its immediacy and force, verbal traces of that force and of the writer's presence inherent in it often continue to haunt the consciousness of the reader. Beckett's Vladimir and Estragon, in one haunted and haunting exchange, speak of "all the dead voices" that "make a noise like wings," "like leaves," "like sand," "like leaves." These may be the voices of actually dead writers that, like ghosts, stalk through the corridors of the mind, appearing and disappearing endlessly. For a while "there" and "then" are realized as "here" and "now."

Writers of course are also readers, and would not otherwise have become writers. In fact, the two activities sufficiently overlap that we may say all readers, including Vladimir and Estragon, are also writers. They are elegists who acknowledge all the dead voices, and as readers so are we all. Beckett was once challenged by someone who said that his vagabonds speak as if they have PhDs, and his answer was, "How do you know they don't?" A good answer. Formal education is not the issue. Every consciousness is thronged with words, fancy or plain, creatively active or relatively quiescent. Among people for whom verbal expression is an urgent need, the very notion of self or identity seems inseparable from the word arrangements they are always recalling and remaking.

Of course human beings are bodies too, and bodies die in a nonmetaphorical sense. Some neurologists are now telling us that in a complicated way we think *with* our bodies, and that may be the case. We also, in good measure, think *about* our bodies and about their eventual death. Writing and reading are forms of resistance to this knowledge. We can think about death and make creative use of such thinking. But we cannot really grasp our inability to think at all. We cannot grasp with language a nothing or silence (for "nothing," and "silence" are just further words) that lies beyond language. The imagining of the end of life for the post-Enlightenment poet—and particularly for the contemporary poet—is a response to that challenge.

Notes

Chapter 1. Imagining the End of Life

1. The Kaddish may have originated from the Catholic idea of Purgatory that became a contested issue during the religious wars of the Renaissance. See Stephen Greenblatt, *Hamlet in Purgatory*, 7–9.

2. Two very helpful sources on the subject of death in ancient Greek art and thought are Emily Vermeule, *Aspects of Death in Early Greek Art and Poetry*, and Robert Garland, *The Greek Way of Death*.

3. In the Anglo-Saxon "Battle of Maldon," God is thanked for remembered *worldly* joys, hence the petitioned grace ("geunne," literally "good") is equally Christian and pagan. Again, in the great tapestries created at the end of the medieval period we find a freewheeling mixture of classical and biblical imagery.

4. See Dudley Fitts, *Poems from the Greek Anthology in English Paraphrase*, 118, 131.

5. Coetzee, *Elizabeth Costello*, 77.

6. Freud, "Thoughts for the Times on War and Death," in *Standard Edition of the Complete Psychological Works*, 14:289.

7. Laforgue, "L'Impossible," in Flores, ed., *An Anthology of French Poetry*, 386–87; Pasolini, "The Day of My Death," in McClatchy, ed., *The Vintage Book of Contemporary World Poetry*, 56; Hardy, *The Mayor of Casterbridge*, 409.

8. Wittgenstein, "Tractatus" (6.431–6.4312), in *The Wittgenstein Reader*, 30.

9. Wittgenstein's analysis calls to mind a character in Mann's *The Magic Mountain* who attempts to console a dying friend by explaining that death is merely an objective event, not one we experience subjectively. The difference is that the novelist is ironically rendering the insensitivity of a well-meaning rationalist, whereas the philosopher queries this rationalism on logical grounds.

10. Burke, "Thanatopsis for Critics: A Brief Thesaurus of Death and Dying," 368–70.

11. Quoted in Enright, ed., *Oxford Book of Death*, 36.

12. Since one cannot record the last moment of one's own life, the occasional attempt of novelists to present a character doing so is a tour de force. Beckett, for example, arranges that the last breath of his Malone will coincide exactly with the last move of his pencil sliding down the page. A different trick is used by Nabokov in *The Real Life of Sebastian Knight,* a novel that at one point leads us to expect a unique self-description of dying, then frustrates our expectation in a surprising way.

13. Heidegger, *Introduction to Metaphysics,* 1.

14. Thomas Nagel reviewed a book that claimed Wittgenstein's support for the argument that language cannot handle such a proposition as "there could have been nothing." He himself backs off a bit from this argument, observing that Wittgenstein's view was not so destructive of religious language as this implies, yet it did affirm language's limited reach. See Nagel's review in the *Times Literary Supplement,* 7 May 2004, 3. See also Wittgenstein, *Lectures and Conversations on Aesthetics, Psychology, and Religious Belief,* 56.

15. Quoted in Kalstone, *Five Temperaments,* 201.

16. Ramazani, *The Poetry of Mourning,* xi.

17. Bromwich, *Skeptical Music,* 6–7. Of Bishop's "The Monument," he writes, for example: "the object of the poem is to compel our attention without giving reasons" (118).

18. See by Ariès: *The Hour of Our Death,* 614; *Western Attitudes toward Death,* 85; "Reversal of Death," 134–58.

19. In Rousset, "La philosophie devant la mort," 174.

20. Paul Robinson, "Five Models for Dying," 91. David Stannard similarly acknowledges that modern man's view of death "is a response to the secularization of the religious universe [and] a consequence of the modern ordering of the social structure. . . . When individuals face death [today] they most often do so with a sense of its meaninglessness and of their own insignificance." In Stannard, ed., *Death in America,* ix, xi.

21. Freud wrote: "There is scarcely any other matter upon which our thoughts and feelings changed have so little since the very earliest times . . . as that of our relation to death" (*Standard Edition,* 17:241–42). I think his intent focus on the psychological aspect of the matter prevents Freud from giving due weight to changes of style in the expression of these feelings and thoughts.

22. Ariès, *Images of Man and Death,* 266. Octavio Paz observes, similarly, that, although man is a symbol-making animal, all that is left for him today, without faith in a future, is "scattered signs." See Paz, *Convergences,* 121.

23. Ariès, *Images of Man and Death,* 268.

24. Hofmannstahl, "Death and the Fool," 136–37.

25. Milosz, *The Witness of Poetry,* 55.

26. Abbott, *Beckett Writing Beckett,* 32–42.

27. Paz, *Convergences,* 123, 129.

28. Heaney, *The Redress of Poetry,* 83.

29. Rilke's letter is reprinted in Ellmann and Feidelson, eds., *The Modern Tradition*, 190–92.

30. Rilke, in *The Essential Rilke*, 83, 15.

31. Stamelman, *Lost Beyond Telling*, 35.

32. Stewart, *Death Sentences*, 316.

33. Cited in Enright, *Oxford Book of Death*, 39.

34. Ramazani, *W. B. Yeats and the Poetry of Death: Elegy, Self-Elegy, and the Sublime*.

35. Some poems by John Donne (for example, the sonnet beginning "At the round earth's imagined corners") *seem* to mourn the self. But the focus in these is on the self's sin, not its mortality. I will have more to say in later chapters on the near-exceptions to my argument presented by such religious poetry.

Chapter 2. Seeding the Idea of Existential Death

1. Ariès, *Western Attitudes toward Death*, 55.

2. Lucien Febvre, in his classic study *The Problem of Unbelief in the Sixteenth Century*, argued that Rabelais was not an atheist because he *could not* have been: social customs were still embraced by Christian authority, and, more fundamentally, the conceptual vocabulary required to support unbelief was not yet in place. Even if this claim is modified (as it should be, for the sixteenth is the first of the modern centuries in which the topic of atheism becomes a subject for debate), it remains suggestive.

3. Huizinga, *Autumn of the Middle Ages*, 156–57.

4. Ibid., 158.

5. The effective translation is by Galway Kinnell. See Villon, *Poems*.

6. Cited with English translation in Speller, *Following Hadrian*, 262.

7. My translation. I have tried to convey the distinctive charm of the French text, which begins, "Amelette Ronsardelette / Mignonelette, doucelette, / Treschere hostesse de mon corps / Tu descens là bas faiblette."

8. This translation is by Arthur Goldhammer. In Chartier, ed., *Passions of the Renaissance*, vol. 3 of *A History of Private Life*, 368–69.

9. Ariès, introduction to *Passions of the Renaissance*, ed. Roger Chartier, vol. 3 of *A History of Private Life*, 1.

10. Quoted in Wayne Booth, *Art of Growing Older: Writers on Living and Aging*, 232.

11. Joel Fineman, *The Subjectivity Effect in Western Literary Tradition*; Harold Bloom, *Shakespeare: The Invention of the Human*; Stephen Greenblatt, "The Making of Hamlet," 43.

12. Donne, *Complete English Poems*, 490.

13. Ariès, introduction to *Passions of the Renaissance* 2–4.

14. Mandeville, *Fable of the Bees*. A French translation was published in 1740.

15. Rousseau, *Emile*, 5, 244.

16. For an interesting discussion of the dispute between Rousseau and Voltaire regarding the Lisbon earthquake of 1755, see Susan Neiman, *Evil in Modern Thought*, 36–40, 137–38.

17. The connection between conscience and natural feeling is easier to make in French, where "conscience" means something close to consciousness or sentiment of being, than in English, where it denotes a faculty that judges and opposes feeling. The word helps Rousseau fuse what is natural and what is moral.

18. Jean Starobinski's *Jean-Jacques Rousseau* develops this idea. See also Gordon, "D. H. Lawrence's Dual Myth of Origin," 238–45.

19. Rousseau, *Emile*, 22.

20. Rousseau, *Julie ou la nouvelle Héloise*, 6:505. My translation.

21. Meltzer, *Natural Goodness of Man*, 216.

22. Rousseau, *Social Contract*, xv.

23. Rousseau, *Social Contract*, chap. 7.

Chapter 3. Opposing the Void

1. Berlin, *The Sense of Reality*, 170–77.

2. Quoted in Porter, *Flesh in the Age of Reason*, 450. Confirming the spirit of this quotation, Shelley, in his preface to "Julian and Maddalo," a poem featuring a philosophic debate between Shelley-Julian and Byron-Maddalo, noted his friend's "intense apprehension of the nothingness of human life." See his *Complete Poems*, 209.

3. Potocki, *Manuscript Found in Saragossa*, 503.

4. This distinction between terror and horror is based on a statement in Radcliffe's posthumously published article, "On the Supernatural in Poetry": "Terror and horror are so far opposite, that the first expands the soul, and awakens the faculties to a high degree of life; the other contracts, freezes, and annihilates them." Quoted in Radcliffe, *Mysteries of Udolpho*, ix.

5. Radcliffe, *Udolpho*, chap. 6.

6. Although it seems unsophisticated, Maturin's novel is really more inward than many later ones it spawned.

7. See Leopardi, *A Leopardi Reader*. His energetic but rationalistic denial that the prospect of death need be fearful is well illustrated by the argument of the Mummies in his "Dialogue between Frederic Ruysche and his Mummies."

8. Hartman, "Romance of Nature and the Negative Way," 40.

9. Frank D. McConnell, ed., *Byron's Poetry*. Other quotations from *Manfred* use this source.

10. Byron wrote to John Murray, his publisher: "Pray, was Manfred's speech to *the Sun* retained in Act third? I hope so: it was one of the best in the thing." Quoted in McConnell, *Byron's Poetry*, 153n.

11. The line was omitted by Murray, apparently at the urging of one of Byron's friends. See McConnell, *Byron's Poetry*, 159n and 150n.

12. Lessing, *Gesammelte Werke*, 3:229:30. My translation.

13. Letter of 3 November 1821 to Murray. Quoted in Steffan, ed., *Lord Byron's Cain*, 9.

14. Atkins, "[Survey of the Faust Theme]," 581–82.

15. See Goethe, *Sämtliche Werke*, vol. 19.

16. Mary Shelley, *Frankenstein*, xi.

17. Bloom, afterword to *Frankenstein*, by Mary Shelley, 215.

18. *Frankenstein*, 95–96.

19. Emily Brontë, *Wuthering Heights*, 290. Heathcliff prefaced this narration to Nelly Dean by saying he had "a strong faith in ghosts." A preternatural experience is being described, kept just within naturalistic limits.

20. Brontë, *Poems*, 102, 120–21.

21. The novel hints at the idea that he may be responsible for Hindley's death through an act of force. John Sutherland examines the evidence, and, while admitting it is ambiguous, is inclined to take the hint seriously. See Sutherland, *Is Heathcliff a Murderer?* 53–58.

22. Ariès, *Hour of Our Death*, 443.

23. Editor's preface to the 1850 edition, quoted in Brontë, *Wuthering Heights*, 364.

Chapter 4. Modifying the Void

1. Hopkins, *Selected Poetry and Prose*, 61.

2. Nietzsche, *The Gay Science*, #125.

3. Rorty, *Contingency, Irony, and Solidarity*, 20.

4. James Knowles, "A Personal Reminiscence," in Tennyson, *Tennyson's Poetry*, 578.

5. Quoted by Robert W. Hill Jr. in Tennyson, *Tennyson's Poetry*, 610.

6. The quoted phrases are from "God and the Universe," *In Memoriam*, and "Vastness."

7. Quoted in Tennyson, *Tennyson's Poetry*, 671.

8. Hallam Tennyson, *Alfred Lord Tennyson: A Memoir by His Son*, 1:321.

9. Ibid.

10. Dwight Culler, *Poetry of Tennyson*, 25.

11. Willey, in Tennyson, *In Memoriam*, 172.

12. Mattes, *"In Memoriam": The Way of a Soul*, 98.

13. Quoted in Tennyson, *Tennyson's Poetry*, 578.

14. Quoted by Browne in *The Power of Place: Charles Darwin*, 188. Tennyson made a similar remark to his son Hallam (*Memoir*, 1:322): "[Evolution] makes no difference to me. . . . To God all is present. He sees present, past, and future as one."

15. Quoted in Tennyson, *Tennyson's Poetry*, 628.

16. Ryals, in Tennyson, *In Memoriam*, 240.

17. Ricks, *Tennyson*, 228.

18. Ryals works out the pattern of this identification in Tennyson, *In Memoriam*, 237–45.

19. In Tennyson, *Tennyson's Poetry*, 578. Very similar is the statement quoted by

Hallam Tennyson (*Memoir* 1:321): "If you allow a God, and God allows this strong interest and universal yearning for another life, surely that is in a measure a presumption of truth."

20. Hill, in Tennyson, *Tennyson's Poetry*, 283n.

21. The poet's self-description according to Knowles. See Tennyson, *Tennyson's Poetry*, 579.

22. Ricks cites both Smith and Langbaum in his *Tennyson*, 133, 131.

23. Hallam Tennyson, *Memoir*, 1:320.

24. Ricks (*Tennyson*, 123) cites Henry James's descriptive phrase and adds his own.

25. This kind of indirection in the imagining of life's end is characteristic of Tennyson's age. Dickens was also protective of Christianity but obliquely, in response to agnostic pressures. Garrett Stewart cites the example of the saintly Betty Higden accompanied in her last moments by Lizzie Hexam, the heroine of *Our Mutual Friend*: "Lizzie Hexam very softly raised the weather-stained grey head, and lifted her as high as Heaven." He describes this as "a suggested transcendence that needs no religious validation" and speaks in general of "the ordinary agnosticism of Dickensian dying . . . qualified by the flavor of augury but not . . . of divination." (See Stewart, *Death Sentences*, 13, 92.) An apparent exception is the death of Paul Dombey, which elicits from the narrator a screed against an unbelieving modern age that no longer acknowledges the truth of immortality. But Dickens's very vehemence in this case reveals the doubts of his age.

26. This observation is developed by H. Porter Abbott in *Beckett Writing Beckett*, 32–42.

27. Ricks, *Tennyson*, 314. He adds pertinently, "Six times [the poem] speaks of 'I' and 'me,' yet no poem was ever less self-absorbed."

28. Culler singles out these faults in *Tennyson*, 246.

29. Quoted in Tennyson, *Tennyson's Poetry*, 496n. See also Hallam Tennyson, *Memoir*, 2:367.

30. Anderson, *Dickinson's Poetry*, 258.

31. Kazin, *God and the American Writer*, 150.

32. The numbers in parentheses throughout this essay, preceded by the pound sign, are based on Dickinson, *The Complete Poems*, edited by Thomas H. Johnson. A later (1998) edition of the poems by Ralph Franklin assigns different numbering, but most critics to date use Johnson's, and Franklin's numbering can easily be matched to it through the index of first lines.

33. I count twenty-seven of these, numbered in Johnson's edition as follows: 18, 185, 216, 237, 324, 338, 357, 376, 401, 432, 437, 455, 489, 501, 508, 576, 597, 797, 817, 1144, 1207, 1258, 1461, 1545, 1589, 1601 and 1751. Dickinson regarded her distance from formal belief with some regret but understood that this distance was connected with her literary gift. On the death of George Eliot, she commented (*Letters*, 700): "The gift of belief which her greatness denied her . . . I trust she receives in the childhood of the kingdom of heaven."

34. Dickinson, *Letters*, 346. Subsequent references to the letters will be indicated parenthetically in the text with an "L" followed by the page number.

35. Kazin, *God and the American Writer*, 146.

36. McNeil, *Dickinson*, 23.

37. Brontë, *Poems*, 120. Some critics find remarkable the male point of view implied in this image of mooring. But a woman may well shelter in a man as a boat moors in a harbor. One recalls Tennyson's beautiful and male-spoken line in *The Princess*—"slip into my bosom and be lost in me"—which Dickinson probably knew.

38. Citing another poem, Anderson writes: "Arrogance is Dickinson's inspired word for defining the hostile encounter between life and death, the absoluteness of the distance between them." See his *Dickinson's Poetry*, 237–38.

39. McNeil comments perceptively on the difference between Dickinson's and Emerson's uses of figurative language. See her *Dickinson*, 63–64 and 133–34.

40. Eberwein, *Emily Dickinson: Strategies of Limitation*, 19.

41. Kazin, *God and the American Writer*, 147.

42. The loaded gun image that appears in one of Dickinson's letters also suggests a distinction between the potential and actual power of words: "an earnest letter is or should be a life warrant or death warrant, for what is each instant but a gun, harmless because 'unloaded,' but that touched goes off" (L663).

43. For Eberwein (*Dickinson*, 219), the King signifies Christ, but for Anderson (*Dickinson's Poetry*, 232), "the King is physical death, not God." In support of Anderson's view, I would add that Dickinson associates royal imagery ("crown," "majesty") with death in #98 and #1691.

44. Judith Farr asserts that the central theme of Dickinson's vision is "time in eternity and eternity in time." This states too abstractly what is presented to us as an experience with shock value. See Farr, *Passion of Emily Dickinson*, 333.

45. Jarrell, "Texts from Housman," in Ricks, ed., *A. E. Housman*, 59.

46. Ibid., 61.

47. All the poems cited are found in *The Collected Poems of A.E. Housman*. Where the poet does not provide titles, I refer to particular poems either by their first lines or by volume title and the assigned numeral.

48. *Last Poems*, IX. This poem is often referred to by its opening line, "The chestnut casts his flambeaux."

49. *A Shropshire Lad*, XXX.

50. *More Poems*, XVI, as it appears in the original edition of 1936.

51. One surmises from the "Note on the Text" supplied by John Carter to *The Collected Poems* that it was he who deleted these asterisks. The key sentences of his statement are these: "The text of [*A Shropshire Lad* and *Last Poems*] presents no problems. [*More Poems* and *Additional Poems*], printed from the author's manuscript remains, are in a somewhat different case. Opportunity was taken, when *The Collected Poems* was being prepared, to make some corrections from the surviving manuscripts." Further information about the publishing history of these poems may be found in John Sparrow, "The Housman Dilemma," in Ricks, ed., *Housman*, 163–75.

52. *More Poems,* XXVII.

53. It was moved from the second (1912) printing of *The Green Helmet* to *Responsibilities,* published in 1914, perhaps because Yeats thought of it as belonging to a volume that reflected a new level of seriousness. According to Foster (*Yeats,* 2:490), it fuses his interest in the dreamlike and ghostly with "his desperate looking back at where his life had gone [in view of] his lacerating sense of his failure with Gonne."

54. The Wild Hunt was a widely circulated folk myth, and the versions of it that Yeats probably had in mind specified a group of demonic huntsmen, sometimes including dead souls, that rush madly across the skies and roads.

55. The intricacies of the relationship are well detailed in two recent biographies: Terence Brown's *Life of Yeats* (especially chapter 4) and R. F. Foster's two-volume *Yeats: A Life.* Both biographies indicate that the relationship was marked throughout by a pattern of advances and retreats. Each party feared to get too close, but neither could give up the other. She needed his worldly influence. He, in turn, needed a feminine ideal that embodied not only beauty but also inviolability.

56. Bloom, *Yeats,* 174.

57. Harwood, quoted in Brown, *Life of Yeats,* 49.

58. Quoted in Foster, *Yeats,* 1:285.

59. Yeats, *Letters.* This letter is dated 1902. It continues: "[Nietzsche] completes Blake [and reading him gives me] the same curious astringent joy."

60. Donoghue, *William Butler Yeats,* 53–56.

61. Quoted in Enright, *Oxford Book of Death,* 179.

62. Dorothy Wellesley's recollection of a conversation with Yeats about the time he was writing *Purgatory* illustrates his interest in this old religious idea. "I asked him: 'What do you believe happens to us immediately after death?' He replied: 'After a person dies he does not realize that he is dead.' I: 'In what state is he?' W.B.Y.: 'In some half-conscious state.' I said: 'Like the period between waking and sleeping?' W.B.Y.: 'Yes.' I: 'How long does this state last?' W.B.Y.: 'Perhaps some twenty years.' 'And after that,' I asked, 'what happens next?' He replied: 'Again a period which is Purgatory. The length of that phase depends upon the sins of the man when upon this earth.'" Quoted in Vendler, *Later Plays,* 195.

63. Yeats, *Mythologies,* 332.

64. Quoted in Foster, *Yeats,* 2:353.

65. Moore wrote: "a goldsmith's bird is as much nature as a man's body, especially if it only sings of what is past or passing or to come to Lords and Ladies." Yeats replied that in writing the later "Byzantium" he took this consideration into account. See Bridge, ed., *Yeats and Moore: Their Correspondence,* 162, 164.

66. Vendler, *Later Plays,* 111.

67. Parkinson, *Yeats: Self-Critic and the Later Poetry: Two Volumes in One,* 2:50–51.

68. Foster, *Yeats,* 2:612. Foster usefully reminds us that the offensive eugenic motif, in a phrase like "best bred of the best," is found in poems that pre-date the influence

of European fascism, such as "Upon a House Shaken by the Land Agitation" and "To a Wealthy Man" (*Yeats*, 2:630).

69. Siegel, ed., *Purgatory: Manuscript Materials*.

70. Yeats, *Oedipus at Colonus*, in *Collected Plays*, 359; Fitzgerald, trans., *Sophocles: Oedipus at Colonus*, 147.

71. Siegel, *Purgatory*, 5.

72. Vendler, *Later Plays*, 199.

73. Whitaker, *Swan and Shadow*, 272. Whitaker distinguishes between the old man's nihilism and Yeats's own desire, but this nihilism has a literal quality that we don't find in the apocalyptic poems.

74. Vendler's comment on an earlier purgatorial play (*Later Plays*, 194) sharply illuminates *Purgatory* as well: "The main difficulty with *The Dreaming of the Bones* is that there is no necessary connection between the lovers and the young man. When 'principles of the mind' are projected into dramatic personages, conflicts that are understandable as interior struggles run the risk of seeming artificial dramatic situations. The vacillation of the young man between the 'sweet wandering snare' of sympathy and his political hatred is insufficiently connected with the transgression of Diarmuid and Dervorgilla. This criticism can in fact be made general, and applies to all [Yeats's] dramatic projections of the purgative process."

75. Peter Ure describes well the "pretty entanglement" Yeats constructed in the argument of *Purgatory*: "The remorseful spirit must, in order to be free, repeat, explore, or dream through the crime which it committed during life; but in this case the renewal of the act . . . renews the self-degrading pleasure that accompanied it. Thus the very consequence from which release is sought—self-degradation—is entailed upon the mother's spirit each time she lives through her transgression." There is, in short, no way the Old Man could have helped her. See Ure, *Yeats the Playwright*, 107.

76. Lawrence, *Complete Poems*, 126.

77. "Gladness of Death," in *Complete Poems*, 677.

78. *Complete Poems*, 255–61.

79. Lawrence, *Women in Love*, 9, 44.

80. Paul Eggert, "The Biographical Issue," in Fernihough, ed., *Cambridge Companion to D. H. Lawrence*, 167.

81. Becket, *Lawrence: Thinker as Poet*, 24.

82. *Sons and Lovers* (chap. 7) illustrates Lawrence's early metaphorical practice: "[Paul Morel] swung negligently . . . as if he were lying on some force. 'Now I'll die,' he said in a detached, dreamy voice, as though he were the dying motion of the swing."

83. Lawrence, *Women in Love*, 61.

84. Lawrence, *Fantasia of the Unconscious*, 121.

85. *Women in Love*, chap. 15.

86. *Complete Poems*, 280–81.

87. Bell, *Lawrence: Language and Being*, 230n, 78, 93.

88. *Complete Poems*, 349–51.

89. Ibid., 697.

90. Helen Sword, "Lawrence's Poetry," in Fernihough, *Cambridge Companion to D. H. Lawrence*, 132.

91. This change apparently cost Lawrence a struggle because in an earlier poem, "Purple Anemones," he portrays Pluto as Persephone's master, allowing her to escape from hell once a year so that he might have the pleasure of hunting her down again. I suspect that the rape idea appealed to him but was overruled by his good sense when he revised "Bavarian Gentians."

92. The revised "Bavarian Gentians" is in *Complete Poems*, 697; the original is on page 960. For further commentary on Lawrence's revision of this poem, see: Gilbert, *Acts of Attention*, 293–99; Sword, in Fernihough, *Cambridge Companion to D. H. Lawrence*, 133–34.

Chapter 5. The Meaningless Void

1. Heaney, *Redress of Poetry*, 137.

2. Foster, *Yeats*, 2:419.

3. Stevens, *Collected Poetry and Prose*, 460. Subsequent quotations from Stevens cite this edition.

4. For an interesting comparison and contrast between Moore's and Bishop's modes of defense, see Diehl, *Elizabeth Bishop and Marianne Moore*, 59–66.

5. Schwartz and Estess, eds., *Bishop and Her Art*, 295.

6. Kalstone, examining Bishop's notebook entries in *Becoming a Poet*, is particularly perceptive concerning her rendering of interiority.

7. Bishop, *Complete Poems*. Subsequent quotations are taken from this edition.

8. Parker, *The Unbeliever*, 36.

9. Kalstone, *Five Temperaments*, 22. He applies this insight to her poem "Over 2000 Illustrations and a Complete Concordance": "[its last line] carries a mysterious yearning to stop observing, which it also guards against." Ibid., 27.

10. Schwartz and Estess, *Bishop and Her Art*, 298.

11. Quoted in Diehl, *Elizabeth Bishop and Marianne Moore*, 33.

12. Motion, *Larkin*, 446.

13. Larkin, *Required Writing*, 47.

14. Ibid., 67.

15. These and subsequent verse quotations are taken from Larkin, *Collected Poems*.

16. In 1954, the editor J. D. Scott christened a new school of writers (including Kingsley Amis and John Wain, whom Larkin had known at Oxford) as "The Movement." By the mid-1960s, another editor, Robert Conquest, was able to characterize the school as featuring "plain language, the absence of posturings, a sense of proportion, humour, abandonment of the dithyrambic ideal." (See Motion, *Larkin*, 242, 265.) Although one understands why Larkin was associated with The Movement, almost each part of this characterization, applied to him, needs altering.

17. Motion, *Larkin*, 224.

18. Heaney, *Redress of Poetry*, 152.

19. One is not surprised to learn from Motion's biography (208) that the phrase "next, please" carried a charge of personal humiliation for Larkin. According to his sister, it was "a phrase he dreaded hearing as a child whenever he reached the head of a queue at school or in shops: it meant he would shortly have to speak, which would be embarrassing because of his stammer."

20. Larkin, *Selected Letters* (10 February 1973), 473.

21. It does so in two extraordinarily good lines: "An only life can take so long to climb / Clear of its wrong beginnings, and may never." This suggests that some people like himself, those who live with "wrong beginnings," may have a harder time than others in facing death.

22. Heaney, *Redress of Poetry*, 146–63.

23. Motion, *Larkin*, 468.

24. Milosz, *Witness of Poetry*, 43. The Nobel Prize was awarded him in 1980, shortly before these lectures were delivered and published.

25. Milosz, *Collected Poems*, 173.

26. Milosz, *Witness of Poetry*, 48–49.

27. Ibid., 14.

28. Here are two examples of his diffidence, culled from *The Collected Poems*: "I thought that all I could do would be done better one day" (202); "Desiring greatness, able to recognize it in others . . . yet I knew what was left for smaller men like me" (451).

29. Milosz, *Collected Poems*, 208.

30. Milosz, *Witness of Poetry*, 16.

31. Milosz, "If There Is No God," 34.

32. Milosz, *Collected Poems*, 441.

33. Milosz, *Witness of Poetry*, 57.

34. Milosz, *Collected Poems*, 323.

35. Milosz's work is full of tender evocations of "my sweet European homeland" and my "Faithful mother tongue." Without the latter, he muses, "who am I? / Only a scholar in a distant country" (*Collected Poems*, 105, 216).

36. *New Yorker*, 19 and 26 August 2002, 76.

37. Milosz, *To Begin Where I Am: Selected Essays*, 320.

38. Her friend Robert Creeley described her as "flooded with purpose," "a wonderfully explicit human." In Levertov, *Selected Poems*, xvi.

39. Williams "was for me the primary influence on my own development" (Levertov, *New and Selected Essays*, 3). Her fullest appreciation of Williams as man and poet appears in the last two essays of *The Poet in the World*.

40. The quotations refer respectively to "First Love," "From Below," and "For the Asking"—all published in Levertov, *The Great Unknowing: Last Poems*.

41. Levertov, *New and Selected Essays*, 16.

42. Levertov, *Conversations with Denise Levertov*, xvi.

43. Levertov's tender feelings for her parents will be apparent in the poems I will soon refer to. For information about the biographical basis of these, beyond what is provided by an afterword in *Selected Poems*, see "Autobiographical Sketch" (*New and Selected Essays*, 258–64) and the early pages of *Tesserae: Memories and Suppositions*.

44. Paul A. Lacey, in Levertov, *Selected Poems*, 203–4.

45. From "The Opportunity," in *Evening Train*. This poem was not included in *Selected Poems*.

46. Levertov, *Selected Poems*, 202.

47. Ibid., 186.

48. Ibid., 34.

49. Levertov, *A Door in the Hive*, 40.

50. This inference is supported by the passion of Levertov's political protests in the 1960s and 1970s, and specifically by her horror of cruelty. Her extensive and recently published correspondence with Robert Duncan, whom she regarded as a mentor, broke up, in fact, over their differences about protesting the Vietnam War. See Gelpi and Bertholf, eds., *Letters of Robert Duncan and Denise Levertov*. See also her political polemics in the latter half of *The Poet in the World*.

51. Levertov wryly describes her complex background (*New and Selected Essays*, 260): "Among Jews a Goy, among Gentiles (secular or Christian) a Jew or at least half Jew which was good or bad according to their degree of anti-semitism), among Anglo-Saxons a Celt . . . among school children a strange exception whom they did not know whether to envy or mistrust. . . . I so often feel English . . . in the United States, while in England I sometimes feel American."

52. One of her late poems, it must be admitted, shows the influence of her conversion by retreating to an older metaphysical position. It celebrates "the mystery / that there is anything . . . rather than void" and praises the "Lord, / Creator, Hallowed One" for sustaining it. See "Primary Wonder" in *Selected Poems*, 192.

53. The poem appears in *The Darkness and the Light* (2001). Perhaps, along with *Millions of Strange Shadows* (1977), it is Hecht's best volume of verse.

54. One notable exception is "Green: An Epistle" from *Millions of Strange Shadows*. Its speaker feels almost a stranger to himself upon realizing he has found peace after a long and too familiar experience of hate and resentment.

55. Hecht, interview, "Distilling the Music of Poetry."

56. In *Obbligati: Essays in Criticism*, Hecht admits to having discovered retrospectively "an unexpected coherence" in the disparate essays. Although he adds he had better leave others to say what this consists of, he is probably referring to a kind of "religious seriousness" that he finds in poets like Dickinson and Bishop (though suspecting that Bishop "would firmly repel" the idea of being a religious poet). His diffidence, however, is noteworthy. See *Obbligati*, viii, 117, 122.

57. Hecht, *On the Laws of the Poetic Art*, xvi.

58. Hecht, *Melodies Unheard*. The last essay is significantly titled "The Music of Forms."

59. Graham, *Swarm*, 35.

60. Graham, *Never*, 84.

61. An experimental poet whose influence Graham has acknowledged, Susan Howe (born 1937), describes "what poetry is" on the cover of her book *Pierce-Arrow*: "It is the blanks and gaps that to me actually represent what poetry is . . . as if there's a place and might be a map to thought when we know there's not."

62. It may not be irrelevant to remark that Graham's self-presentation at a recent reading was buoyant, spirited, and distinctly youthful. I have noticed also that two earlier volumes of her work give her birth year as 1950, whereas two later volumes give it as 1951—a trivial bit of vanity but one that accords with the picture of a playful rather than solemn persona that I find in her work.

63. Graham, *Dream of the Unified Field*, 74.

Bibliography

Abbott, H. Porter. *Beckett Writing Beckett: The Author in the Autograph.* Ithaca: Cornell University Press, 1996.

Anderson, Charles. *Emily Dickinson's Poetry: Stairway of Surprise.* New York: Holt, Rinehart, and Winston, 1960.

Ariès, Philippe. *The Hour of Our Death.* Translated by Helen Weaver. New York: Alfred A. Knopf, 1981.

———. *Images of Man and Death.* Translated by Janet Lloyd. Cambridge: Harvard University Press, 1985.

———. Introduction to *The Passions of the Renaissance,* edited by Roger Chartier. Vol. 3 of A History of Private Life,. Cambridge: Belknap Press of Harvard University Press, 1989.

———. "Reversal of Death: Changes in Attitudes to Death in Western Societies." Translated by Valerie M. Stannard. In *Death in America,* edited by David Stannard. Philadelphia: University of Pennsylvania Press, 1975.

———. *Western Attitudes toward Death from the Middle Ages to the Present.* Translated by Patricia M. Ranum. Baltimore: Johns Hopkins University Press, 1974.

Atkins, Stuart. "[Survey of the Faust Theme]." In *Faust: A Tragedy by Johann Wolfgang von Goethe.* 2d ed. Translated by Walter Arndt and Cyrus Hamlin. New York: W. W. Norton and Co., 2001.

Becket, Fiona. *D. H. Lawrence: The Thinker as Poet.* London and New York: Macmillan/St. Martin's, 1977.

Bell, Michael. *D. H. Lawrence: Language and Being.* Cambridge: Cambridge University Press, 1992.

Berlin, Isaiah. *The Sense of Reality: Studies in Ideas and Their History.* Edited by Henry Hardy. New York: Farrar, Straus, and Giroux, 1996.

Bishop, Elizabeth. *The Complete Poems.* New York: Farrar, Straus, and Giroux, 1980.

Bloom, Harold. *Genius: A Mosaic of One Hundred Exemplary Creative Minds.* New York: Warner Books, 2002.

———. *Shakespeare: The Invention of the Human.* New York: Riverhead Books, 1998.

———. *Yeats.* New York: Oxford University Press, 1970.

Booth, Wayne. *The Art of Growing Older: Writers on Living and Aging.* Chicago: University of Chicago Press, 1992.

Bridge, Ursula, ed. *W. B. Yeats and T. Sturge Moore: Their Correspondence 1901–1937.* London: Routledge and Kegan Paul, 1953.

Bromwich, David. *Skeptical Music: Essays on Modern Poetry.* Chicago: University of Chicago Press, 2001.

Brontë, Emily. *Poems.* Edited by Philip Henderson. London: Lawson and Dunn, 1947.

———. *Wuthering Heights.* Edited by Ian Jack. Oxford and New York: Oxford University Press. 1991.

Brown, Terence. *The Life of W. B. Yeats.* Oxford: Blackwell, 1999.

Browne, Janet. *The Power of Place: Charles Darwin: The Origin and After: The Years of Fame.* New York: Alfred A. Knopf, 2002.

Burke, Kenneth. "Thanatopsis for Critics: A Brief Thesaurus of Death and Dying." *Essays in Criticism* (1952): 368–70.

Byron, George Gordon, Lord. *Byron's Poetical Works.* Oxford: Oxford University Press, 1967.

Chartier, Roger, ed. *The Passions of the Renaissance.* Vol. 3 of *A History of Private Life,* edited by Philippe Ariès and Georges Duby; translated by Arthur Goldhammer. Cambridge: Belknap Press of Harvard University Press, 1987–91.

Coetzee, J. M. *Elizabeth Costello.* New York: Viking, 2003.

Culler, Dwight. *The Poetry of Tennyson.* New Haven: Yale University Press, 1977.

Dickinson, Emily. *The Complete Poems of Emily Dickinson.* Edited by Thomas H. Johnson. Boston: Little, Brown, and Company, 1960.

———. *Letters of Emily Dickinson.* 3 vols. Edited by Thomas H. Johnson. Cambridge: Harvard University Press, 1970.

Diehl, Joanne Feit. *Elizabeth Bishop and Marianne Moore: The Psychodynamics of Creativity.* Princeton: Princeton University Press, 1993.

Donne, John. *The Complete English Poems.* Edited by C. A. Patrides. New York and Toronto: Alfred A. Knopf, 1991.

Donoghue, Denis. *William Butler Yeats.* New York: Viking, 1971.

Eberwein, Jane Donahue. *Emily Dickinson: Strategies of Limitation.* Amherst: University of Massachusetts Press. 1985.

Ellmann, Richard, and Charles Feidelson, eds. *The Modern Tradition.* New York: Oxford University Press, 1965.

Enright, D. J., ed. *The Oxford Book of Death.* Oxford: Oxford University Press, 2002.

Farr, Judith. *The Passion of Emily Dickinson.* Cambridge: Harvard University Press, 1992.

Febvre, Lucien. *The Problem of Unbelief in the Sixteenth Century: The Religion of Rabelais.* Translated by Beatrice Gottlieb. Cambridge: Harvard University Press, 1982.

Fernihough, Anne, ed. *The Cambridge Companion to D. H. Lawrence.* Cambridge: Cambridge University Press, 2001.

Fineman, Joel. *The Subjectivity Effect in Western Literary Tradition: Essays toward the Release of Shakespeare's Will*. Cambridge: MIT Press, 1991.

Fitts, Dudley. *Poems from the Greek Anthology in English Paraphrase*. New York: New Directions, 1941.

Fitzgerald, Robert, trans. *Sophocles: Oedipus at Colonus*. In vol. 2 of *The Complete Greek Tragedies*, edited by David Grene and Richard Lattimore. Chicago: University of Chicago Press, 1960.

Flores, Angel, ed. *An Anthology of French Poetry from Nerval to Valéry*. Garden City, N.Y.: Doubleday Anchor, 1958.

Foster, R. F. *Yeats: A Life*. 2 vols. Oxford: Clarendon Press, 1997–2003.

Freud, Sigmund. *Standard Edition of the Complete Psychological Works of Sigmund Freud*. Translated by James Strachey, in collaboration with Anna Freud, Alix Strachey, and Alan Tyson. 24 vols. London: Hogarth Press, 1957–74.

Garland, Robert. *The Greek Way of Death*. Ithaca: Cornell University Press. 1985.

Gelpi, Albert, and Robert J. Bertholf, eds. *The Letters of Robert Duncan and Denise Levertov*. Stanford: Stanford University Press, 2004.

Gilbert, Sandra M. *Acts of Attention: The Poems of D. H. Lawrence*. Ithaca: Cornell University Press, 1972.

Goethe, Johann Wolfgang von. *Gespräche mit Eckermann*. In *Sämtliche Werke*, vol. 19. Munich: Carl Hanser, 1986.

Gordon, David J. "D. H. Lawrence's Dual Myth of Origin." In *Critical Essays on D. H. Lawrence*, edited by Dennis Jackson and Fleda Brown Jackson. Boston: G. K. Hall and Co., 1988.

Graham, Jorie. *The Dream of the Unified Field: Selected Poems 1974–1994*. Hopewell, N.J.: Ecco Press, 1994.

———. *The Errancy*. Hopewell, N.J.: Ecco Press, 1997.

———. *Never*. Hopewell, N.J.: Ecco Press, 2002.

———. *Swarm*. Hopewell, N.J.: Ecco Press, 2000.

Greenblatt, Stephen. *Hamlet in Purgatory*. Princeton: Princeton University Press, 2001.

———. "Hamnet's Death and the Making of Hamlet." *New York Review of Books*, 21 October 2004, 42–47.

Hardy, Thomas. *The Mayor of Casterbridge*. London: Penguin Books, 1985.

Hartman, Geoffrey H. "The Romance of Nature and the Negative Way." In *Modern Critical Views: William Wordsworth*, edited by Harold Bloom. New York: Chelsea House, 1985.

Heaney, Seamus. *The Redress of Poetry*. New York: Farrar, Straus, and Giroux, 1995.

Hecht, Anthony. *The Darkness and the Light*. New York: Alfred A. Knopf, 2001.

———. "Distilling the Music of Poetry." Interview with Dinitia Smith. *New York Times*, 21 January 2003.

———. *Flight from the Tombs*. New York: Alfred A. Knopf, 1996.

———. *On the Laws of the Poetic Art*. Princeton: Princeton University Press, 1995.

————. *Melodies Unheard: Essays on the Mysteries of Poetry.* Baltimore: Johns Hopkins University Press, 2003.

————. *Millions of Strange Shadows.* New York: Alfred A. Knopf, 1977.

————. *Obbligati: Essays in Criticism.* New York: Atheneum Books, 1989.

————. *Venetian Vespers.* New York: Alfred A. Knopf, 1979.

Heidegger, Martin. *An Introduction to Metaphysics.* Translated by Ralph Manheim. New Haven: Yale University Press, 1997.

Hofmannstahl, Hugo von. "Death and the Fool." In *Poems and Verse Plays,* translated by Michael Hamburger. New York: Pantheon Books, 1961.

Hopkins, Gerard Manley. *Selected Poetry and Prose.* Harmondsworth: Penguin Books, 1954.

Housman, A. E. *The Collected Poems of A. E. Housman.* New York: Holt, Rinehart, and Winston, 1965.

Howe, Susan. *Pierce-Arrow: Poems.* New York: New Directions, 1999.

Huizinga, Johan. *The Autumn of the Middle Ages.* Translated by Rodney J. Payton and Ulrich Mammetzsch. Chicago: University of Chicago Press, 1996.

Kalstone, David. *Becoming a Poet: Elizabeth Bishop, Marianne Moore, Robert Lowell.* New York: Farrar, Straus, and Giroux. 1989.

————. *Five Temperaments: Elizabeth Bishop, Robert Lowell, James Merrill, Adrienne Rich, John Ashbery.* New York: Oxford University Press, 1977.

Kazin, Alfred. *God and the American Writer.* New York: Alfred A. Knopf, 1997.

Larkin, Philip. *Collected Poems.* Edited by Anthony Thwaite. New York and London: Farrar, Straus, and Giroux, and Marvell Press, 1989.

————. *Selected Letters of Philip Larkin 1940–1985.* Edited by Anthony Thwaite. London: Faber and Faber, 1992.

————. *Required Writing: Miscellaneous Pieces 1955–1982.* London: Faber and Faber. 1983.

Lawrence, D. H. *The Complete Poems of D. H. Lawrence.* Edited by Vivian de Sola Pinto and F. Warren Roberts. New York: Penguin Books. 1984.

————. *Fantasia of the Unconscious/Psychoanalysis of the Unconscious.* London: Penguin Books, 1977.

————. *Women in Love.* Edited by David Farmer, Lindeth Vasey, and John Worthen. London: Penguin Books, 1995.

Leopardi, Giacomo. *A Leopardi Reader.* Edited and translated by Ottavio M. Casale. Urbana: University of Illinois Press, 1981.

Lessing, Gotthold Ephraim. "Wie die Alten den Tod gebildet." In *Gesammelte Werke,* vol. 3. Munich: Carl Hanser, 1982.

Levertov, Denise. *Conversations with Denise Levertov.* Edited by Jewel Spears Brooker. Jackson: University of Mississippi Press, 1996.

————. *A Door in the Hive.* New York: New Directions, 1989.

————. *Evening Train.* New York: New Directions, 1992.

————. *New and Selected Essays.* New York: New Directions, 1997.

————. *Poems: 1960–1967.* New York: New Directions, 1967.

————. *The Poet in the World*. New York: New Directions, 1973.

————. *Selected Poems*. Preface by Robert Creeley. Afterword by Paul A. Lacey. New York: New Directions, 2002.

————. *Tesserae: Memories and Suppositions*. New York: New Directions, 1995.

Mandeville, Bernard. *The Fable of the Bees and Other Writings*. Edited by E. J. Hundert. Indianapolis: Hackett Publications, 1997.

Mattes, Eleanor B. *"In Memoriam": The Way of a Soul*. New York: Exposition Press, 1951.

Maturin, Charles Robert. *Melmoth the Wanderer*. Lincoln: University of Nebraska Press. 1966.

McClatchy, J. M., ed. *The Vintage Book of Contemporary World Poetry*. New York: Random House, 1996.

McConnell, Frank D., ed. *Byron's Poetry*. New York: W. W. Norton and Co., 1978.

McNeil, Helen. *Emily Dickinson*. London: Virago Press, 1986.

Meltzer, Arthur M. *The Natural Goodness of Man: On the System of Rousseau's Thought*. Chicago: University of Chicago Press, 1990.

Milosz, Czeslaw. *The Collected Poems 1931–1987*. New York: HarperCollins, 1988.

————. "Eyes." *New Yorker*, 19 and 26 August 2002, 76.

————. "If There Is No God." *New Yorker*, 30 August 2004, 34.

————. *To Begin Where I Am: Selected Essays*. New York: Farrar, Straus, and Giroux, 2001.

————. *The Witness of Poetry*. Cambridge: Harvard University Press, 1983.

Motion, Andrew. *Philip Larkin: A Writer's Life*. New York: Farrar, Straus, and Giroux, 1993.

Nagel, Thomas. Review of *Why There Is Something Rather Than Nothing*, by Bede Rundle. *Times Literary Supplement*, 7 May 2004, 3.

Neiman, Susan. *Evil in Modern Thought: An Alternative History of Philosophy*. Princeton: Princeton University Press, 2002.

Nietzsche, Friedrich. *The Gay Science*. Translated by Walter Kaufmann. New York: Vintage, 1974.

Parker, Robert Dale. *The Unbeliever: Poetry of Elizabeth Bishop*. Urbana and Chicago: University of Illinois Press, 1988.

Parkinson, Thomas. *"W. B. Yeats, Self-Critic: A Study of His Early Verse" and "The Later Poetry."* (Two works combined in a single volume.) Berkeley and Los Angeles: University of California Press, 1971.

Paz, Octavio. *Convergences: Essays on Art and Literature*. Translated by Helen Lane. San Diego: Harcourt Brace Jovanovich, 1987.

Porter, Roy. *Flesh in the Age of Reason*. London: Allen Lane, 2003.

Potocki, Jan. *The Manuscript Found in Saragossa*. Translated by Ian Maclean. New York: Viking, 1995.

Radcliffe, Ann. *The Mysteries of Udolpho: A Romance*. Introduction by Bonamy Dobrée. Oxford: Oxford University Press, 1966.

Ramazani, Jahan. *The Poetry of Mourning: The Modern Elegy from Hardy to Heaney*. Chicago: University of Chicago Press, 1994.

———. *W. B. Yeats and the Poetry of Death: Elegy, Self-Elegy, and the Sublime*. New Haven: Yale University Press, 1990.

Ricks, Christopher. *Tennyson*. New York: Macmillan, 1972.

———, ed. *A. E. Housman: Twentieth-Century Views*. Englewood Cliffs, N.J.: Prentice-Hall, 1968.

Rilke, Rainer Maria. *The Essential Rilke*. Selected and translated by Galway Kinnell and Hannah Liebmann. New York: HarperCollins, 2000.

Robinson, Paul. "Five Models for Dying." *Psychology Today*, March 1981, 85–91.

Ronsard, Pierre de. *Pièces posthumes: Les derniers vers*. In *Oeuvres complètes*, 2:634–37. Paris: Bibliothèque de la Pléiade, 1950.

Rorty, Richard. *Contingency, Irony, and Solidarity*. Cambridge and New York: Cambridge University Press, 1990.

Rousseau, Jean-Jacques. *Emile*. Translated by Barbara Foxley. New York: Everyman Library, 1969.

———. *Julie ou la nouvelle Héloïse*. Paris: Garnier-Flammarion. 1967.

———. *Reveries of the Solitary Walker*. Translated by Peter France. New York: Penguin, 1984.

———. *The Social Contract and Discourse on the Origin of Inequality*. Edited with an introduction by Lester G. Crocker. New York: Washington Square Press, 1971.

Rousset, Bernard, "La philosophie devant la mort." In *La mort aujourd'hui*, edited by L. V. Thomas, B. Rousset, and T. V. Thao. Paris: Editions Anthropos, 1977.

Sachs, Hanns. *The Creative Unconscious: Studies in the Psychoanalysis of Art*. Cambridge, Mass.: Sci-Art Publishers, 1951.

Schwartz, Lloyd and Sybil Estess. *Elizabeth Bishop and Her Art*. Ann Arbor: University of Michigan Press, 1983.

Siegel, Sandra F., ed. *Yeats's Purgatory: Manuscript Materials Including the Author's Final Text*. Ithaca: Cornell University Press. 1986.

Shelley, Mary. *Frankenstein or The Modern Prometheus*. Afterword by Harold Bloom. New York: New American Library, 1965.

Shelley, Percy. *The Complete Poems of Percy Bysshe Shelley*. New York: Modern Library, 1994.

Speller, Elizabeth. *Following Hadrian: A Second-Century Journey through the Roman Empire*. New York: Oxford University Press. 2003.

Stamelman, Richard. *Lost Beyond Telling: Representations of Death and Absence in Modern French Poetry*. Ithaca: Cornell University Press, 1990.

Stannard, David, ed. *Death in America*. Philadelphia: University of Pennsylvania Press, 1975.

Starobinski, Jean. *Jean-Jacques Rousseau: La transparence et l'obstacle*. Paris: Librairie Plon, 1957.

Steffan, Truman Guy, ed. *Lord Byron's Cain: Twelve Essays with a Text and Variants*. Austin: University of Texas Press, 1968.

Stevens, Wallace. *Collected Poetry and Prose.* Edited by Frank Kermode and Joan Richardson. New York: Library of America, 1997.

Stewart, Garrett. *Death Sentences: Styles of Dying in British Fiction.* Cambridge: Harvard University Press, 1984.

Sutherland, John. *Is Heathcliff a Murderer? and Other Puzzles in Nineteenth-Century Fiction.* Oxford and New York: Oxford University Press, 1996.

Tennyson, Alfred, Lord. *"In Memoriam": Alfred, Lord Tennyson.* Edited by Robert H. Ross. New York: W. W. Norton and Co., 1973.

———. *Tennyson's Poetry.* Edited by Robert W. Hill Jr. New York: W. W. Norton Co., 1971.

Tennyson, Hallam. *Alfred Lord Tennyson: A Memoir by His Son.* 2 vols. New York: Macmillan, 1897.

Ure, Peter. *Yeats the Playwright: A Commentary on Character and Design in the Major Plays.* London: Routledge and Kegan Paul, 1963.

Vendler, Helen Hennessey. *Yeats's "Vision" and the Later Plays.* Cambridge: Harvard University Press, 1963.

Vermeule, Emily. *Aspects of Death in Early Greek Art and Poetry.* Berkeley and Los Angeles: University of California Press, 1979.

Villon, François. *The Poems of François Villon.* Translated by Galway Kinnell. New edition. Hanover, N.H.: University Press of New England, 1977.

Whitaker, Thomas. *Swan and Shadow: Yeats's Dialogue with History.* Chapel Hill: University of North Carolina Press, 1964.

Wittgenstein, Ludwig. *Lectures and Conversations on Aesthetics, Psychology, and Religious Belief.* Compiled from notes taken by Yorick Smythies, Rush Rhees, and James Taylor. Edited by Cyril Barrett. Berkeley and Los Angeles: University of California Press, 1972.

———. *The Wittgenstein Reader.* Edited by Anthony Kenny. Oxford: Blackwell, 1994.

Yeats, W. B. *The Collected Plays of W. B. Yeats.* New York: Macmillan, 1952.

———. *The Collected Poems of W. B. Yeats.* New York: Macmillan, 1955.

———. *The Letters of W. B. Yeats.* Edited by Allan Wade. New York: Macmillan, 1955.

———. *Mythologies.* New York: Collier-Macmillan, 1959.

Acknowledgments

The author gratefully acknowledges permission to quote from the following works:

"Cootchie" and "The Unbeliever" from *The Complete Poems: 1927–1979* by Elizabeth Bishop, copyright © 1979, 1983 by Alice Helen Methfessel.

"The Lovers" (14 lines) from *The Dream of the Unified Field: Poems 1974–1994* by Jorie Graham, copyright © 1995 by Jorie Graham. Reprinted by permission of HarperCollins Publishers, Inc. "The Guardian Angel of Self-Knowledge" (5 lines) and "Against Eloquence" (entire) from *The Errancy* by Jorie Graham, copyright © 1997 by Jorie Graham. Reprinted by permission of HarperCollins Publishers, Inc.

Excerpt from "Apprehensions" in *Collected Earlier Poems* by Anthony Hecht, copyright © 1990 by Anthony E. Hecht. Used by permission of Alfred A. Knopf, a division of Random House, Inc. "The Darkness and the Light Are Both Alike to Thee" from *The Darkness and the Light: Poems* by Anthony Hecht, copyright © 2001 by Anthony E. Hecht. Used by permission of Alfred A. Knopf, a division of Random House, Inc.

"Aubade," "High Windows," and excerpt from "The Old Fools" from *Collected Poems* by Philip Larkin, copyright © 1988, 2003 by the Estate of Philip Larkin. Reprinted by permission of Farrar, Straus and Giroux, LLC.

"Bavarian Gentians" by D. H. Lawrence, "The Ship of Death" by D. H. Lawrence, from *The Complete Poems of D. H. Lawrence* by D. H. Lawrence, edited by V. de Sola Pinto and F. W. Roberts, copyright © 1964, 1971 by Angelo Ravagli and C. M. Weekley, Executors of the Estate of Frieda Lawrence Ravagli. Used by permission of Viking Penguin, a division of Penguin Group (USA) Inc. The poem "Bavarian Gentians" (23 lines) and the poem "The Ship of Death" (10-line excerpt) from *The Complete Poems of D. H. Lawrence* by D. H. Lawrence, edited by V. de Sola Pinto and F. W. Roberts, copyright © 1964, 1971 by Angelo Ravagli and C. M. Weekley, Executors of

Index of Names and Works

David J. Gordon is professor emeritus of English at Hunter College and the Graduate School of the City University of New York. Among his previous books are *D. H. Lawrence as a Literary Critic, Iris Murdoch's Fables of Unselfing,* and *Literary Atheism.*